KidsOwn Worship™:

FaithWeaver Children's Church

leader guide • winter 2000-2001

FaithWeaver
Children's Church

www.faithweaver.com

Group
Loveland, Colorado

KidsOwn Worship™: FaithWeaver™ Children's Church, Leader Guide, Winter 2000-2001
Copyright © 2000 Group Publishing, Inc.

First printing, 2000

Visit our Web site: **www.grouppublishing.com**

Credits

Contributing Authors: Janet R. Reeves, Amy Simpson, Bonnie Temple, and April I. Thoms
Editors: Lori Haynes Niles, Beth Rowland, and Bonnie Temple
Creative Development Editors: Karl Leuthauser, Dave Thornton, and Paul Woods
Chief Creative Officer: Joani Schultz
Copy Editor: Alison Imbriaco
Art Director: Jenette L. McEntire
Cover Art Director: Debbie Collins
Cover Designer: Debbie Collins
Computer Graphic Artist: Anita M. Cook
Cover Photographer: Bohm-Marrazzo
Illustrator: Dana Regan
Production Manager: Peggy Naylor

ISBN 0-7644-1040-7
Printed in the United States of America.

10 9 8 7 6 5 4 3 2 1   02 01 00

Contents

Welcome to KidsOwn Worship™: FaithWeaver Children's Church

"From the lips of children and infants you have ordained praise" (Psalm 8:2a).

Kids need to praise and worship God just as adults do. KidsOwn Worship™ is about kids worshipping God. We call it "active reflection." We say "active" because kids need to be involved in worship as full participants. It's not enough for kids to sit in rows and watch what's happening at the front of the room. They need to encounter God with their minds, to worship God with their actions, and to praise God with their mouths. And it needs to be fun!

We say "reflection" because worship is about reflecting on the character and deeds of a good God. KidsOwn Worship is not just a time to learn more about the Bible, though that happens throughout the worship sessions. The primary focus of KidsOwn Worship is introducing kids to who God is and worshipping God through praise, music, Scripture, activities, and prayer.

Essential Components of KidsOwn Worship

KidsOwn Worship includes a unique combination of materials that will help you lead kids in worshipping God. In the KidsOwn Worship Kit, you'll find these items:

• **A Leader Guide**—In this book, you'll find all the information you need to make your children's church run smoothly. The book contains detailed instructions for all thirteen worship sessions, along with hints and tips to make it easy. In the back of the leader guide, you'll find the song lyrics and motions for all the worship songs you'll use during the quarter. You might consider tearing out the lyrics pages and keeping them in a separate folder. That way, you can pull out just the lyrics pages you need for each week.

• *Songs From FaithWeaver, Vol. 6* **CD**—Each quarter you'll have a split-channel CD with more than twenty worship songs that have been chosen because kids love them and because they tie in with the themes of the worship sessions. The music includes the best of contemporary Christian music, as well as traditional hymns of the faith. You'll find special helps in the leader guide to help you explain the words and concepts of these songs in language kids understand. Every song provides an opportunity to understand God more and to praise God for who he is and what he does. A Lyrics Transparencies packet is included in the KidsOwn Worship Kit to help kids learn the words.

• *KidsOwn Worship Video*—*KidsOwn Worship Video* is a collection of short video segments that explain a character trait of God's, illustrate a Scripture passage, or help children worship through prayer or music. These video segments are used as discussion-starters and worship tools. The video is a powerful way to get kids thinking about God.

• **Worship-Starter Stuff**—In each quarter's KidsOwn Worship Kit, you'll also find several items that are designed to add the "wow" factor to your worship time with kids. In the kit, you might find chemicals for a science experiment, sun-sensitive paper, clay that doesn't get hard until it gets wet, memory foam, or ingredients to make rubber balls. These items are chosen because they intrigue kids. And if kids are intrigued, they'll be excited about what they're learning about God and worship.

• **KidsOwn Worship Skits**—Also in the KidsOwn Worship Kit, you'll find a booklet of thirteen puppet scripts for use with the preschoolers or other young children in your worship group. The skits feature Theophilus the FaithRetriever™. Theo is a golden retriever puppy whose name means "lover of God." Theo's adventures will help you teach the preschoolers in your group to love God. The skits are written to tie in with each week's worship theme. Theophilus puppets are available at your local Christian bookstore.

Tips for Using KidsOwn Worship

Whether you have fifteen kids or one hundred and fifty kids in your children's church, you can use KidsOwn Worship with fantastic results. These tips will help you set up your program and make it easy to run.

How the Program Works

KidsOwn Worship works well with both preschoolers and elementary children. Putting children of different ages in the same worship setting has many benefits. It teaches kids that the church is a community; the older children learn to help the younger children, and the younger children learn from the examples the older children set. Also, having all children in the same worship setting means you need fewer volunteers and fewer classrooms.

For most of the worship session, you'll want to keep all children of all ages together. But during the middle section of the worship session—Let's Learn the Point!—you have the option of having the preschoolers meet separately. That's because we recognize that preschoolers and elementary children learn on different levels. Having the children learn in two groups allows you to really target the different intellectual levels.

Flip through this leader guide. You'll notice that, in the middle of each session, there's a tear-out page titled "Preschool Activities." For every week, we've included twenty-five minutes of activities that apply directly to preschoolers. If you choose to have a separate preschool classroom for a portion of the worship time, tear out this page each week, and give it to the preschool leader.

We made this curriculum flexible to serve your needs. As you flip through this leader guide, you'll see that the first page of each session includes a chart with all the activities planned for the worship session. Notice the two columns in the middle of the chart. The left column is labeled, "Let's Learn the Point! Preschool Activities." The right column is labeled, "Let's Learn the Point! Elementary Activities."

If you choose to separate the children into two groups, you can check this chart to see what activities each group will be doing each week. But notice that there are asterisks before some of the activity titles.

Three activities in each session (the ones preceded by asterisks) are designed to work well with kids of all ages. If you prefer to keep all your children, preschoolers and elementary kids, in the same room for the entire worship time, plan to use these three asterisked activities.

A Look at the Session

Session Sequence	What Children Will Do	Supplies
Getting Started	Find a warm welcome at children's church.	KidsOwn Worship Kit: Songs From FaithWeaver, Vol. 6 Classroom Supplies: CD player
1 Let's Praise God! (up to 25 minutes)	Sing: • "Joy!" (track 5) • "That You May Believe" (John 20:31) (track 20) • "Rise Up and Praise Him" (track 14) • "For Us a Child Is Born" (Isaiah 9:6) (track 21) • Your Everlasting Love" (track 17)	KidsOwn Worship Kit: Songs From FaithWeaver, Vol. 6; Lyrics Transparencies Classroom Supplies: CD player, overhead projector, copy of Isaiah's script (p. 7)

2 Let's Learn the Point!	PRESCHOOL ACTIVITIES (up to 25 minutes)		2 Let's Learn the Point!	ELEMENTARY ACTIVITIES (up to 25 minutes)	
What Children Will Do	**Supplies**		**What Children Will Do**	**Supplies**	
The Promised Savior—Play a game about God's promise to send a Savior	Classroom Supplies: CD player, CD of praise music		✱ Tales of the Future— Watch a video about prophecy.	KidsOwn Worship Kit: KidsOwn Worship Video: "Tales of the Future" Classroom Supplies: TV, VCR	
Christmas Trees—Plant "Christmas trees" and talk about Jesus' family tree.	Classroom Supplies: Paper cups, potting soil, evergreen sprigs, curling ribbon, scissors, pens		✱ The Righteous Branch— Look at prophecies about Jesus and put together a Christmas tree.	Classroom Supplies: Artificial Christmas tree, Bibles, paper, pencils	
God's Promises Came True—Tell good things about Jesus and sing a song about God's promises.			✱ A Great Light—Discuss prophecies about Jesus, and hang Christmas lights on the Christmas tree.	Classroom Supplies: Bible, Christmas lights, paper, markers, scissors	

Session Sequence	What Children Will Do	Supplies
3 Let's Pray! (up to 10 minutes)	The Offering—Give their offerings and thank God for sending a Savior.	KidsOwn Worship Kit: Songs From FaithWeaver, Vol. 6: "We Believe in God" (track 10) Classroom Supplies: CD player, offering bowls
	Praise Cheer—Praise God for keeping his promise to send a Savior.	
	Just Like You Promised—Sing a song as a closing prayer.	KidsOwn Worship Kit: Songs From FaithWeaver, Vol. 6: "Just Like You Promised" (track 2) Classroom Supplies: CD player

Setting up the Room

Setting up your worship room doesn't have to be complicated. If you have a choice, choose a large room without permanent seating—a gym or fellowship room would be perfect. This way, kids can sit on the floor. And when you need to reorganize into different-sized project groups, you won't have to waste time moving furniture around. Another plus is that without chairs you can get by with a smaller room than you'd need if you had chairs or pews.

While a big, empty room is an ideal place to meet, don't worry if you're stuck with a meeting area that's less than perfect. If your room has permanent seating, you can have small groups gather at the end or middle of pews. You can have them meet in the aisles, at the front or back of the room, or on the staircase that leads to the balcony. If your room is too big, consider closing off one end with chalkboards or room dividers. If your room is too small, consider using the hallway for small group discussions or consider breaking up the group and meeting at two different times.

You'll need to set up audio-visual equipment in your worship area. For most of the worship sessions, you'll need a TV and VCR, as well as an overhead projector. Set up the TV and VCR at the front of the room. If you have more than seventy-five kids (fifty if your room has permanent seating), consider setting up a second TV on the other side of the room and hooking it into the VCR. This way, all the children will have a screen that's easy to see. Set up the overhead projector so that you can project a large, clear image on the wall. If you can't use a large, light-colored wall, you'll need to set up a screen.

If you have fifty or more children, consider using a sound system and a microphone. It can feel strange and awkward to use a microphone if you aren't used to it. But the benefits are well worth the effort of getting used to it. In a group of fifty or more children, a microphone will ensure that everyone can hear what you're saying. That's really important when you're giving out project instructions. A microphone will also help kids hear the song leader sing the songs. Children are more likely to sing enthusiastically if they can really hear the songs. And a microphone will free you to ask individual children to share their insights and comments with the rest of the group. A microphone is a wonderful tool! Ask the sound people at your church for specific instructions on using your church's system.

You'll probably want to have a stand of some kind for your supplies. Consider using a small table or a couple of black metal music stands. Organizing everything you need to lead the worship session and having what you need at hand will make the worship session go much more smoothly. Stand to the side of the supply table or music stand. Kids will feel more connected to you if you aren't hidden behind a table.

Place a few tables around the perimeter of the room, too. These tables will serve as supply tables and project tables.

If you'd like to take attendance as kids arrive, set up an attendance table near the door. Have a volunteer take attendance as you greet the children. You'll find forms to help you take attendance on pages 10 and 11.

Decorations

KidsOwn Worship is a time to celebrate who God is and what God has done for us. Keep this in mind as you decorate the room. Make the room inviting, colorful, and fun. You may want to put up posters that celebrate God's deeds or show his beautiful creation. You may want to make worship banners to help kids remember that "God Is Love" or that "God Saves Us." Look at the themes of the sessions in this book and make banners or posters that will celebrate those themes. Also, you may want to hang balloons or streamers or other party-type decorations to lend a festive atmosphere to your room.

Staffing Your Children's Church

You'll need to recruit at least one adult helper no matter what size your children's church is. We recommend that you recruit at least one helper for every fifteen children. While you're leading the group from the front of the room, the other helpers can gather supplies, help individual children, help project groups solve problems, and help answer questions. You may even want to rotate the teaching among the adult helpers each week so that no one feels overburdened with the need to prepare and teach.

Song Leader

If you're not comfortable leading the songs, recruit a song leader to help. Tell the song leader that he or she only needs to help for the first twenty-five minutes or so of the worship time. Be sure to give the CD to the song leader, and let him or her know which songs will be sung each week. You may choose to lead the discussion and activities between the songs yourself or you may want the song leader to lead the entire Let's Praise God! time. Be sure to coordinate this with the song leader.

Preschool Leader

KidsOwn Worship is designed to give you the option of teaching the preschoolers separately during a portion of the worship time. Read through the format of a few of the sessions, then decide whether you would prefer to keep all the children together for the entire worship hour or have the preschoolers go to their own classroom for the middle section of activities titled, Let's Learn the Point!

If you decide on a separate class for preschoolers, recruit a preschool leader, and make sure there's a room where the preschoolers can meet. Each week you'll tear out the appropriate Preschool Activities page. Coordinate with the preschool leader when to pick up the children and when to return them to the big group. Also decide with the preschool leader who will collect the supplies the preschoolers will need for their time together.

If Your Children's Church Is Small

If your children's church is made up of thirty or fewer children, you'll be able to run an effective children's church program with a minimum of volunteers. With two leaders, one leader can present material or lead worship songs while the other leader gathers supplies and helps children with their individual needs.

If Your Children's Church Is Large

If you have more than thirty children in your children's group, we suggest that you use a small group format. This will change both the number of volunteers and the kind of volunteers you'll need.

You'll still want at least two adult leaders for your children's church. But in a small group format, you'll form permanent small discussion groups (Praise Crews) of about five children each, and you'll need a responsible teenager or an adult helper for each group.

However, the helpers you'll recruit to head up each small group don't need to feel pressured to teach or to lead the large group. Their responsibility is to build relationships with the kids in their small groups—to make every child feel welcome and important. The Praise Crew Leaders make sure that every child is involved in discussions and that every child has a role in the activities. (See the end of this section for a handout, "What's a Praise Crew Leader?" that will help your small group leaders train for their role.)

The small group format really maximizes the time children spend in children's church. Small groups give kids a relationship connection every week. And small groups give every child a chance to be heard and involved in every discussion and every activity.

Have the small groups sit together during children's church. For fun, you might have each small group choose a name for itself—"God's Mighty Followers" or "Morphin' New Creations in Christ," for example. Anytime there's a discussion, have the children talk in their small groups. You can provide time at the beginning of the worship sessions for children to talk in their groups about how their week went and at the end of the worship sessions for kids to pray together. Every quarter or twice a year, form new small groups so children get to know other children.

Involving Older Children

If you have older elementary children or preteens who want to be involved in children's church, consider forming a children's worship team. It's a great way to help children learn to serve, and you'll find that many children are eager to participate on a worship team. You may want to invite children you think would do a good job, or you may want to ask for volunteers. It doesn't really matter whether the children are great singers; what counts is their enthusiasm for worship.

Help the worship team children learn the song lyrics and song motions by holding regular rehearsals. Then, during your children's church, have the worship team help you lead the rest of the group in singing the praise songs. The worship team leaders can also pass out supplies and lead children in responsive readings or group prayers. They can even help set up the room before worship and clean it up after worship. Be sure to rotate children into the worship team often so many children get a chance to learn how to serve.

Have Fun Worshipping God During KidsOwn Worship!

Above all, never forget that children's church is primarily a time for worship. It's a time to help kids focus on God, learn about God, and honor God for the wonderful things he's done. Children's church should be a time of discovery and joy. It should be a time for praise and exuberant worship. It's a time for kids to get excited about God.

Do whatever you can to encourage children's sense of wonder and awe. Encourage kids to wonder about God, to adore God, and to express their love for God creatively and enthusiastically. And be assured that your efforts in focusing kids' attention on their Creator will have eternal effects!

The FaithWeaver™ Family of Christian Growth Resources

If you enjoy using KidsOwn Worship: FaithWeaver Children's Church, you'll also enjoy using other products in the Faith-Weaver family of Christian growth resources. In addition to the KidsOwn Worship curriculum, the FaithWeaver family includes the following components:

• **FaithWeaver Bible Curriculum**—an exciting Sunday school program for everyone in your church, from infants to adults. The adult Sunday school program includes great ideas to help parents teach their kids about God at home.

• **FW Friends™: Small Groups for Kids**—a fun easy-to-do midweek program encourages Christian growth as kids connect with God, significant mentoring adults, and each other.

• **FaithWeaver HomeConnect™** —resources to help families weave faith into their lives after they leave the church building. Discussions outside of church can powerfully influence children's faith development, and parents can use these resources to begin conversations at home to help family members grow in faith.

• **FaithWeaver PastorConnect™**—practical resources designed to help your church's pastor fully integrate the Faith-Weaver curriculum by incorporating the curriculum's themes into the weekly worship service.

FaithWeaver Bible Curriculum is a tool God will use to change the lives of the children, youth, and adults in your church. Created to be biblically sound, educationally effective, and engaging for every person, FaithWeaver Bible Curriculum will help weave faith into the lives of children and families in your church like no other curriculum can.

Research shows that the most powerful influence on faith development is the conversations about faith that take place in the home. By using all the FaithWeaver Bible Curriculum age levels, you can provide an opportunity for family members to study the same Bible passage every week. As toddlers, children, youth, and adults study the same passages—at different levels, of course—students and families will have something to discuss at home.

Using FaithWeaver, your church will be able to weave together Sunday school, KidsOwn Worship sessions, an FW Friends program, and adult worship. Or you may want to use just the KidsOwn Worship portion of FaithWeaver to further the Christian growth of your church's children and families. It's easy to use, flexible, and powerful! Use it however you want in your ministry to children, youth, or adults. And know that it will impact the lives of all who attend.

Praise Crew Roster

Praise Crew Number: _____

Praise Crew Leader: _____

Praise Crew Members

1. _____

2. _____

3. _____

4. _____

5. _____

Praise Crew Number: _____

Praise Crew Leader: _____

Praise Crew Members

1. _____

2. _____

3. _____

4. _____

5. _____

Praise Crew Number: _____

Praise Crew Leader: _____

Praise Crew Members

1. _____

2. _____

3. _____

4. _____

5. _____

Praise Crew Number: _____

Praise Crew Leader: _____

Praise Crew Members

1. _____

2. _____

3. _____

4. _____

5. _____

Alphabetical Master List

Name	Praise Crew Number	Name	Praise Crew Number

What's a Praise Crew Leader?

If you've been asked to be a Praise Crew Leader, you've met two important qualifications: You love God, and you love kids.

During KidsOwn Worship, you'll meet with a group of about five children every week. **You're not in charge of preparing or teaching activities—you just get to be there and enjoy the children who are a part of your Praise Crew!**

The following guidelines will help you be a successful Praise Crew Leader!

A Praise Crew Leader is

- a friend and a helper
- someone who knows and calls kids by name
- someone who offers kids choices
- someone who encourages kids
- someone who makes sure every kid is involved and having fun

A Praise Crew Leader isn't

- the boss or the teacher
- someone who makes all the decisions
- someone who gives all the answers
- someone who yells at kids or puts them down

When talking with kids,

say,

- Let's keep moving so we can do as many fun activities as possible.
- Listen carefully so you'll know what to do next.
- Stay with us; we need your help in this activity.
- That's a unique way of doing things! How did you think of that? Let's try it this way.
- It's important that we all follow the instructions and work together.
- Please move over here so you can see better.

don't say,

- Stop talking and get back to work.
- Be quiet and listen!
- Don't run around the room.
- You're doing it wrong!
- Don't do that!
- Stay out of that area!

As a Praise Crew Leader, What Will I Do?

• Be early, and be ready to welcome the kids in your Praise Crew! Spend the time before worship begins chatting with the kids in your group. Make every child feel welcome. Make an effort to get to know each child.

• Be an enthusiastic worshipper! Sing the praise songs loud and clear, and do all the motions. The kids in your group will be looking to you as an example. If you put your heart into worshipping God, they will too!

• Listen carefully to the directions you're given. It's your job to help each child participate in the worship activities and the discussion that follows. You need to pay attention so you can keep the kids focused and on task.

• Gently redirect kids who get off track or start misbehaving. Read the next section of this handout for ideas on how to handle several specific problems.

Troubleshooting

Most of the time, things will go smoothly for your Praise Crew, but every once in a while, you may run into a tricky situation. Here's some advice on how to handle different challenges.

If Older Kids Complain About Being With Younger Ones

Highlight their helping role. Encourage them to help younger kids with crafts and other activities. Acknowledge them by telling younger kids, "[Name of older child] is really good at that. Why don't you ask him [or her] to help?"

If I Have a Clique in My Crew

Cliques can make the Praise Crew experience unhappy for the outsiders. Encourage friendships between all crew members by pairing kids with partners they don't know very well during pair-shares or during prayer times.

If a Crew Member Won't Participate

Help shy children feel welcome by calling them by name often and asking them questions directly. Respond to their answers with a smile and an encouraging statement, such as, "That's really interesting" or "Wow! I bet that made you feel special!" Also try giving children special jobs. For example, assign them the task of looking up Scriptures or leading your group in a closing prayer.

If someone doesn't want to participate, that's OK. Remember that everyone can have a bad day now and then. Encourage the child to participate, but if he or she really doesn't want to, just let the child sit with the group quietly. Chances are, when the child sees how much fun everyone else is having, he or she will want to join in too.

If People in My Crew Don't Get Along

Quietly take the children aside. Tell them you've noticed they're not getting along. Let them know that, although they don't have to be best friends, they do need to be respectful and kind to each other. Remind the children that we're here to worship God and that it's hard to worship God when we're thinking bad thoughts about each other.

If I Have an Overly Active Child

Pair up this child with yourself during partner activities, and suggest that he or she sit with you during quiet times. Try to make sitting still a game by saying, "Let's see how long you can sit still without interrupting. I'm timing you. Ready? Go!"

If the child is really uncontrollable, ask the worship leader for advice.

With a little patience and humor, you and your Praise Crew can have an awesome experience at KidsOwn Worship.

OK to copy

1

Prophets Foretell Jesus' Coming

Jeremiah 33:14-16

Worship Theme: God promised to send a Savior.

A Look at the Session

Session Sequence	What Children Will Do	Supplies
Getting Started	Find a warm welcome at children's church.	**KidsOwn Worship Kit:** *Songs From FaithWeaver, Vol. 6* **Classroom Supplies:** CD player
Let's Praise God! 1 *(up to 25 minutes)*	Sing: • "Joy!" (track 5) • "Mary's Boy Child" (track 3) • "That You May Believe" (John 20:31) (track 20) • "Rise Up and Praise Him" (track 14) • "For to Us a Child Is Born" (Isaiah 9:6) (track 21) • "Your Everlasting Love" (track 17)	**KidsOwn Worship Kit:** *Songs From FaithWeaver, Vol. 6;* Lyrics Transparencies **Classroom Supplies:** CD player, overhead projector, copy of Isaiah's script (p. 17)

2 Let's Learn the Point! — PRESCHOOL ACTIVITIES *(up to 25 minutes)*

What Children Will Do	Supplies
The Promised Savior—Play a game about God's promise to send a Savior.	**Classroom Supplies:** CD player, CD of praise music
Christmas Trees—Plant "Christmas trees" and talk about Jesus' family tree.	**Classroom Supplies:** Paper cups, potting soil, evergreen sprigs, curling ribbon, scissors, pens
God's Promises Came True—Tell good things about Jesus and sing a song about God's promises.	

2 Let's Learn the Point! — ELEMENTARY ACTIVITIES *(up to 25 minutes)*

What Children Will Do	Supplies
✳ **Tales of the Future**— Watch a video about prophecy.	**KidsOwn Worship Kit:** *KidsOwn Worship Video:* "Tales of the Future" **Classroom Supplies:** TV, VCR
✳ **The Righteous Branch**— Look at prophecies about Jesus and put together a Christmas tree.	**Classroom Supplies:** Artificial Christmas tree, Bibles, paper, pencils
✳ **A Great Light**—Discuss prophecies about Jesus, and hang Christmas lights on the Christmas tree.	**Classroom Supplies:** Bible, Christmas lights, paper, markers, scissors

✳ Starred activities can be used successfully with preschool and elementary children together.

Customize your session to fit your needs. You can separate preschoolers and elementary children for Section 2.

Or, if you keep the children all together for the entire worship session, we suggest you choose from the starred activities.

Session Sequence	What Children Will Do	Supplies
Let's Pray! 3 *(up to 10 minutes)*	**The Offering**—Give their offerings and thank God for sending a Savior.	**KidsOwn Worship Kit:** *Songs From FaithWeaver, Vol. 6:* "We Believe in God" (track 10) **Classroom Supplies:** CD player, offering bowls
	Praise Cheer—Praise God for keeping his promise to send a Savior.	
	Just Like You Promised—Sing a song as a closing prayer.	**KidsOwn Worship Kit:** *Songs From FaithWeaver, Vol. 6:* "Just Like You Promised" (track 2) **Classroom Supplies:** CD player

Why We Worship

For thousands of years, God reassured people with his promise to send a Savior. The Old Testament is full of prophecies about the promised Savior. God promised that the Savior would bring healing and comfort. God promised that the Savior would be a king from David's family and that he would bring a kingdom of peace and justice. During Advent, we prepare for the coming of the Christ child, and we celebrate the Old Testament prophecies, knowing that each one of them is fulfilled in Jesus. "O come, O come Immanuel, and ransom captive Israel...Rejoice! Rejoice! Immanuel shall come to thee, O Israel."

Bible Background

Jeremiah 33:14-16

This passage was written nearly six hundred years before Jesus was born. The northern kingdom of Israel had fallen to the Assyrians, who had in turn fallen to the Babylonians. Jeremiah also saw the fall of the southern kingdom of Judah to the Babylonians, concluding with the destruction of Jerusalem in 587 B.C.

Despite all that was going on around him, Jeremiah's message in this passage is one of hope. Repeating nearly word-for-word the message he had given in Jeremiah 23:5-6, Jeremiah utters here his most important message about the coming Messiah. This ideal King would be a descendant of David but would rule with more wisdom, justice, and righteousness than any other king had ever done.

This coming Messiah would not only rescue his people from their oppressors, but he would also reunite the kingdoms of Israel and Judah, which had been divided since the death of Solomon more than three hundred years earlier. The people would be restored both physically and spiritually and would look to God as their righteousness (Jeremiah 33:16).

After reading this passage, it's easy to understand why people of Jesus' day expected a Messiah who would lead them in throwing off Roman rule and restoring the united kingdom of Israel. From our standpoint in history, we know that Jesus came first as the suffering servant (see Isaiah 53), drawing people to himself through his perfect life and his message of repentance. One day, however, Jesus will return to complete his fulfillment of Old Testament prophecies and rule as king over all heaven and earth. As we look forward to our celebration of Jesus' birth, we can also look forward to the day that Jesus will return to take those who believe in him to live with him in heaven. That's God's message of hope for Christians in today's broken world!

Skits and Puppets

In the KidsOwn Worship Kit, you'll find a collection of skits titled, "KidsOwn Worship Skits." The skits are designed to be used with Theophilus the FaithRetriever puppet during the preschool activities. You can purchase a Theo puppet at your local Christian bookstore.

Getting Started

Song Lyrics and Motions

To make the worship session go more smoothly, tear out the lyrics sheets in the back of the book and keep them in a separate folder. Each week, pull out only the sheets you need for the day's worship session.

Before Worship

 Set up a TV and VCR, and cue the *KidsOwn Worship Video* to the "Tales of the Future" segment. Watch the segment at least once before the worship session so you'll be familiar with it.

Recruit someone from your congregation to play the part of Isaiah. Photocopy the script on page 17 and give it to your volunteer. Ask the volunteer to rehearse the script several times. Be sure to explain to him when he needs to arrive and how long he'll need to stay. Ask him to wear Old Testament garb.

Arrival Time

Play *Songs From FaithWeaver, Vol. 6* as children arrive. Designate greeters to welcome children at the entrance, and ask your greeters to shake hands with the children and welcome them by name.

 Let's Praise God!

SAY Welcome, everyone! Let's take a moment to greet each other. Today we're going to talk about a very important promise, so, as we're greeting each other, let's talk about promises. Turn to a friend and say, "Hello." Then tell your friend about a promise you made and about a promise that has been made to you.

Give the children a moment to greet each other and talk about promises.

ASK • Why are promises so important?
• How do we feel when people keep their promises to us?

SAY A kept promise makes us happy—it gives us joy. Today we're going to talk about a promise that God made and kept. It was a promise that brought a lot of joy to the whole world. Thousands of years ago God promised to send a Savior to the world. And he did! God kept his promise by sending his Son, Jesus. Let's sing about the joy of that promise.

track 5 Sing "Joy!"
Lyrics and motions are in the back of this book.

SAY The Old Testament is the part of the Bible that comes before Jesus was born. Many books in the Old Testament tell us about God's promise to send a Savior. The Old Testament told people what Jesus would be called, where he would be born, and what he would do. Let's sing "Mary's Boy Child" to celebrate the fact that the Bible tells us about God's promise to send a Savior.

track 3 Sing "Mary's Boy Child!"
Lyrics and motions are in the back of this book.

ASK • Why do you think God promised to send a Savior?
• Why do you think all of God's promises about Jesus are in the Bible?

SAY God really wants us to believe in Jesus. God knows that we need to believe and trust in Jesus to be saved. There's a verse at the end of the book of John that tells us that all the things in that book were written so that we might believe in Jesus. I think that's why all the promises about Jesus were written in the Old Testament. God wanted people to look forward to the Savior, and he wanted to give people ways to know that Jesus was really the Savior. Let's sing!

 Sing "That You May Believe" (John 20:31).
Lyrics and motions are in the back of this book.

ASK • Why was it important for God to send us a Savior?
• Why is it so important for us to believe in Jesus?

SAY Let's praise God for promising to send a Savior to us.

 Sing "Rise Up and Praise Him."
Lyrics and motions are in the back of this book.

SAY Now let's listen to what God said about the promised Savior hundreds of years before he was born.

Invite the person you've recruited to be Isaiah to come in and do a dramatic reading of the script.

> **Isaiah:** My name is Isaiah and I am a prophet of the Lord. This is what the Lord told me would happen.
>
> "Suddenly there will be no more gloom for the land that suffered...Before those people lived in darkness, but now they have seen a great light. They lived in a dark land, but a light has shined on them. God, you have caused the nation to grow and made the people happy...
>
> "A child has been born to us; God has given a son to us. He will be responsible for leading the people. His name will be Wonderful Counselor, Powerful God, Father Who Lives Forever, Prince of Peace.
>
> "Power and peace will be in his kingdom and will continue to grow forever. He will rule as king on David's throne and over David's kingdom. He will make it strong by ruling with justice and goodness from now on and forever. The Lord All-Powerful will do this because of his strong love for his people." (Isaiah 9:1a, 2-3a, 6-7; New Century Version)
>

Say goodbye to "Isaiah."

ASK • What did our Isaiah say about the Savior God promised?
• If you had heard the real Isaiah speak these words hundreds of years before Jesus was born, what would you have thought about the promised Savior?

SAY Let's celebrate the promised Savior, Jesus!

 Sing "For to Us a Child Is Born" (Isaiah 9:6)
Lyrics and motions are in the back of this book.

SAY God promised to send a Savior to us because he loves us so much. Let's sing about God's everlasting love.

 **track 17**   Sing "Your Everlasting Love."
Lyrics and motions are in the back of this book.

PRAY God, your love really is deeper and higher than anything in this world. You loved us so much you promised to send a Savior to save us from our sins. And you kept your promise. Thank you, God. In Jesus' name, amen.

Let's Learn the Point!

PRESCHOOL ACTIVITIES, pp. 19-20

At this time, have the preschool helper invite the preschoolers to go to their own room for this section of activities. Tear out the Preschool Activities page, and give it to the preschool leader. Have the preschool leader bring the preschoolers back to participate in the prayer time with the older children. If you prefer to keep all the children together, do the starred activities. They will work well with both elementary and preschool children. ●●●●●●●●●●➤

ELEMENTARY ACTIVITIES

✻ Tales of the Future

 Play the "Tales of the Future" segment from the *KidsOwn Worship Video*. The video shows various prophecies about the future and that only the prophecies in the Bible can be counted on.

If the children don't already discuss questions in small groups, form groups of two or three children, and have them discuss these questions.

ASK
• Why do you think people are so curious about what the future will be like?
• Why do you think people keep trying to predict the future when they hardly ever predict it accurately?
• What do you think the people thought when God promised to send a Savior?
• It took hundreds of years for God's promises about Jesus to come true. Do you think people started to wonder whether God would keep his promise? Why or why not?
• If God made you a promise, would you believe it? Why or why not?

SAY God knew that people needed a Savior. And, right from the very beginning, God promised the people that a Savior was coming. That Savior is Jesus. Let's learn more about God's promises about Jesus.

✻ The Righteous Branch

You'll need an artificial Christmas tree that comes in numerous pieces.

ASK • Who can tell me what a family tree is?

(continued on page 21)

Worship Leader Tip

The Christmas tree you'll set up today will be used each Sunday between now and Christmas. If possible use a five- to six-foot artificial Christmas tree. If that's not possible, you can make a tree to hang on the wall. Use the illustration in the margin as a guide.

Preschool Activities

Prophets Foretell Jesus' Coming Jeremiah 33:14-16

Worship Theme: God promised to send a Savior.

Using Theo

Consider using Theophilus the FaithRetriever puppet today in these ways:

• Have Theo lead the preschoolers from the main worship area to the preschool room.

• Have Theo pretend to be God during "The Promised Savior" activity.

• See the KidsOwn Worship Kit for a puppet skit written for today's worship session.

The Promised Savior

You'll need a cassette player or CD player and a tape or CD of praise music.

SAY Today we're talking about how God promised to send a Savior to the people. Let's play a game about God's promise.

Choose one child to pretend to be the Savior. Choose another child to pretend to be God. Ask the "Savior" to hide. Ask "God" to help you with the CD player or cassette player.

Explain to the children that they should walk around the room while the music plays, then, when the music stops, everyone should freeze. Have "God" stop the music—or tell you when to stop the music—and say "Do not worry! Do not fear! The promised Savior will soon be here!" Then have the "Savior" come out of hiding and tap each frozen child on the head so he or she can move again. Have all the children clap and cheer for the "Savior."

Choose different children to pretend to be the Savior and God, and play the game again.

After you've played several rounds of the game, gather the children together.

SAY The real God promised many people that he would send a Savior to them. Jesus is the Savior God sent. God kept his promise to send a Savior.

ASK • Do you think the people were happy when Jesus came? Why?

SAY God kept his promise to send Jesus. God always keeps his promises. Let's learn more about Jesus, the promised Savior.

Christmas Trees

You'll need paper cups and potting soil, as well as enough sprigs from an evergreen tree or bush to have one for each child. The sprigs should be six to eight inches long and should be from a soft, non-prickly evergreen. You'll also need curling ribbon in Christmas colors. Curl the ribbon before you cut it into two- to three-inch sections.

Help the children write their names on the bottoms of the paper cups. Then have the children use their hands to scoop potting soil into the paper cups and "plant" the evergreen sprigs so they look like Christmas trees. When the children are finished, have them brush off their hands, or provide wet wipes and have them wipe their hands.

ASK • Do you know what a family tree is?

SAY We use a word-picture called a "family tree" to show that a group of people all belong to the same family.

(continued on page 20)

(continued from page 19)

ASK • Who's in your family?

SAY All the people in your family—your sisters, your brothers, your aunts, your uncles, your cousins and your grandparents—all belong on the same family tree.

The Bible tells us that God promised to send a special person to the world—God promised to send Jesus to us. The Bible says that Jesus was part of a very special family tree. The Bible says that Jesus belongs to King David's family tree. That means that Jesus is a king like David was a king. Before Jesus was born, the Bible promised that Jesus would be a very good king who would always be fair and do the right thing.

ASK • Do you think the promises about Jesus came true?

SAY Let's decorate our trees to show they're special family trees.

Have the children decorate the sprigs by placing bits of curling ribbon between the tiny "branches." Older children will be able to wind the ribbon around the branches.

SAY You can take your little trees home to help you remember that Jesus is from a special family tree. Whenever you see a Christmas tree, remember that God promised that he would send a Savior to the world and that the Savior would be a part of King David's special family tree.

God's Promises Came True

SAY Let's pretend that you're God and you want to tell all the people that Jesus is coming. You want them to know that Jesus is really, really special. Let's think about what we'd say about Jesus if we were God.

Discuss what the children would say about Jesus if they were God. Then play this game. Have the entire group chant, "Hear ye! Hear ye! The Savior is coming. This is what he'll be like." Then have one of the children stand up and say something about Jesus, such as "Jesus will love children" or "Jesus will be kind."

SAY God told the people all those things. God told the people that Jesus was kind and gentle and loving. God told them that Jesus would forgive their sins and would help them. The people were excited and they were impatient while they waited for Jesus. It was just as hard for them to wait for Jesus as it is for us to wait for Christmas. But, finally, Jesus was born. All God's promises came true! Let's sing a song about God's promises coming true.

Sing the following words to the tune of "Oh, Christmas Tree."

At Christmastime, at Christmastime,
God's promises came true.
At Christmastime, at Christmastime,
God's promises came true.
A promised Savior was to come
From good King David's family tree.
At Christmastime, at Christmastime,
God's promises came true.

(continued from page 18)

SAY The Old Testament tells us about the promised Savior's family tree. Listen to these words from the Old Testament, and listen for the clue about Jesus' family tree. "The Lord says, 'The time is coming when I will do the good thing I promised to the people of Israel and Judah. In those days and at that time, I will make a good branch sprout from David's family. He will do what is fair and right in the land' " (Jeremiah 33:14-15, NCV).

ASK • What does this verse tell us about Jesus' family tree?
• What else does this verse tell us about Jesus?

Show the children the Christmas tree pieces.

SAY Today we're going to set up a Christmas tree in our worship area that will remind us about the promised Savior, the righteous branch from King David's family.

Hand out Bibles if the children haven't brought their own. Also hand out paper and pencils. Have the children work in groups of three. If you have adult helpers to work with each group, the groups can be a little bigger—up to five children. Have the groups each look up Isaiah 11:1-5 and make lists of their discoveries about what the Savior would be like. If you have more than ten groups of children, you may want to have some of the groups look up Isaiah 9:6-7.

Give the children three or four minutes to work and discuss. Then give each group a branch to add to the tree. Have each group bring the branch to the tree and attach it. As each group adds its branch to the tree, have those children tell the entire group one characteristic of the promised Savior they discovered in Isaiah 11:1-5. Continue until the Christmas tree is completely assembled.

ASK • Did these promises about the promised Savior come true?
• Why do you think God made so many promises about Jesus?
• How does knowing that Jesus is everything God promised he would be make you feel?

✶ A Great Light

SAY The Old Testament has another prophecy about Jesus. We're going to use this prophecy as we add the first decorations to this tree. Listen while I read from the Old Testament. See if you can discover what decorations we'll add to the tree first.

Read Isaiah 9:2 from an easy-to-understand version of the Bible. Be sure to emphasize the word "light."

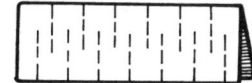

ASK • What do you think we'll put on the tree first?
• In what way is Jesus a light in the darkness?

SAY The New Testament says that Jesus is the light of the world. Jesus is the promised Savior the Old Testament was talking about. Let's decorate our tree with lights.

Recruit two or three older children to put Christmas lights on the tree.

Give the other children paper and markers. Make sure there are scissors available too.

SAY On your piece of paper, write about, or draw a picture of, one of the promises about Jesus that came true.

Once the children have done that, show them how to fold and cut their papers to make paper chains. Follow the instructions in the margin.

SAY When you unfold your piece of paper, notice how it forms a long chain. These chains will remind us of the connection between the Old Testament and the New Testament. God made promises about the Savior in the Old Testament. The New Testament tells us how those promises came true when Jesus was born. Let's decorate the tree with our "promise chains."

Help the children decorate the Christmas tree with the "promise chains." Then plug in the Christmas tree lights. Keep the paper chains away from the light bulbs. And be sure to unplug the lights when you leave the room at the end of the worship session.

 Let's Pray!

The Offering

Gather the children around the Christmas tree.

SAY God promised to send a Savior to us because he loved us and knew that we needed a Savior to save us from our sins. Let's sing while we collect the offering.

 Sing "We Believe in God."
Lyrics and motions are in the back of this book.

Pass the offering bowl while you sing.

Praise Cheer

Teach the children this cheer—the cadence of the second line is twice as fast as the first line.

> **We praise you**
> **'Cause your promises come true!**

Then invite children to come to the front one by one to call out one special thing about the promised Savior, Jesus. After each child shares, have the rest of the group call out the cheer as a joyful prayer.

Just Like You Promised

SAY Let's sing our closing song as a prayer to God.

 Sing "Just Like You Promised"
Lyrics and motions are in the back of this book.

Dismiss the children quietly.

Zechariah Prophesies About Jesus

2

Luke 1:68-79

Worship Theme: God meets our needs.

A Look at the Session

Session Sequence	What Children Will Do	Supplies
⏱ Getting Started	Find a warm welcome at children's church.	KidsOwn Worship Kit: *Songs From FaithWeaver, Vol. 6* Classroom Supplies: CD player
🏠 Let's Praise God! 1 (up to 25 minutes)	Sing: • "The Good Life" (track 11) • "My God Is" (track 4) • "Mary's Boy Child" (track 3) • "Joy to the World!" (track 1) • "Just Like You Promised" (track 2) • "For to Us a Child Is Born" (Isaiah 9:6) (track 21) • "Jesus Is Lord of All" (track 9) • "I Love You, Lord" (track 18)	KidsOwn Worship Kit: *Songs From FaithWeaver, Vol. 6;* Lyrics Transparencies Classroom Supplies: CD player, overhead projector

2 Let's Learn the Point! — PRESCHOOL ACTIVITIES (up to 25 minutes)

What Children Will Do	Supplies
The Shape of Love—Hold felt shapes representing God's love, and hear the Bible story.	Classroom Supplies: Red and green felt, scissors
Blanket of Love—Make a blanket as a reminder that God loves us and meets our needs.	Classroom Supplies: Fabric, "The Shape of Love" felt pieces, safety pins, glitter glue, glue gun
✱ **Full Hearts**—Decorate and eat heart-shaped cookies to remind them that God meets our needs.	Classroom Supplies: Heart-shaped cookies, frosting, plastic knives, decorations, napkins

2 Let's Learn the Point! — ELEMENTARY ACTIVITIES (up to 25 minutes)

What Children Will Do	Supplies
✱ **Surprise Visitor**—Hear a surprise visitor tell Zechariah's story.	Classroom Supplies: Copy of "Zechariah's Story" (p. 33), costume, poster board, scissors, markers
✱ **The Amazing Needomatizer**—Watch a video and discuss how God provides for our needs.	KidsOwn Worship Kit: *KidsOwn Worship Video:* "The Amazing Needomatizer" Classroom Supplies: TV, VCR
Worship Banners—Make banners to praise God for meeting our needs.	KidsOwn Worship Kit: *Songs From FaithWeaver, Vol. 6:* "Joy to the World!" (track 1) Classroom Supplies: Bibles, CD player, poster board, scissors, markers, craft supplies, masking tape

Session Sequence	What Children Will Do	Supplies
🙏 Let's Pray! 3 (up to 10 minutes)	**The Offering**—Write ways God has met their needs, and thank him.	Classroom Supplies: Offering bowls, envelopes, pencils
	Lord, Help Us See—Ask God to show them needs to pray for.	Classroom Supplies: Candle, matches
	Christmas Prayer Tree—Pray for needs by writing them on ornaments and hanging them on a Christmas tree.	KidsOwn Worship Kit: *Songs From FaithWeaver. Vol. 6:* "Just Like You Promised" (track 2) Classroom Supplies: CD player, pencils, wrapping paper, scissors, ornament hooks, Christmas tree

✱ Starred activities can be used successfully with preschool and elementary children together.

Customize your session to fit your needs. You can separate preschoolers and elementary children for Section 2.

Or, if you keep the children all together for the entire worship session, we suggest you choose from the starred activities.

Session 2 • KidsOwn Worship   23

Why We Worship

When Zechariah's son, John, was born, Zechariah was filled with the Holy Spirit and began to praise God and to prophesy. In his prophecy, Zechariah pointed out specific ways the Savior, Jesus, would meet the needs of people. He would bring salvation and forgiveness, hope, and help in following God.

Whether we admit it or not, we all need God. We need the help and the salvation that only Jesus offers. It's tempting to think people or things can meet our needs, but time proves both to be temporary and empty. Only God can truly meet our deepest needs, and he's waiting to do just that. That's reason to worship!

Skits and Puppets

In the KidsOwn Worship Kit, you'll find a collection of skits titled, "KidsOwn Worship Skits." The skits are designed to be used with Theophilus the FaithRetriever puppet during the preschool activities. You can purchase a Theo puppet at your local Christian bookstore.

Bible Background

Luke 1:68-79

The priest Zechariah doubted an angel's message to him that his aging wife, Elizabeth, would have a son who would prepare the way for the Lord. Because of his unbelief, Zechariah was struck with an inability to speak until the baby was born. Shortly after appearing to Zechariah, the angel appeared to Mary, telling her that she would give birth to the Messiah and that Mary's cousin, Elizabeth, was also pregnant. Mary visited Elizabeth, who by then was expecting the child who would become John the Baptist. Mary proclaimed her good news to Elizabeth and glorified the Lord for his goodness to her and to all the earth (see Luke 1:46-56).

When John was born, Zechariah was suddenly able to speak again. Filled with the Holy Spirit, Zechariah delivered the prophecy contained in Luke 1:68-79. This proclamation is known as Benedictus, which is the Latin for "praise be," the first words of the prophecy.

Luke 1:76 indicates that John would be a prophet who would prepare the way for Jesus. He would be the Elijah figure mentioned in Malachi 4:5-6, who was to appear before the coming of the Lord. John was to give people the knowledge of salvation. They had drifted so far away from God that they had lost even that knowledge. John was to prepare them for Jesus by reminding them of what that salvation was all about—the remission of sins.

How would the remission of sins be made possible? Through the mercy of God. The words of Luke 1:78-79 are reminiscent of Isaiah 60:1: "Arise, shine, for your light has come, and the glory of the Lord rises upon you." The coming of Jesus would bring light to a dark world, through the mercy of our loving God.

The final promise of peace mentioned at the end of verse 79 might have brought a sigh of relief to the average Jew. Having suffered and struggled so much, the Jews longed for peace. Our world is no different. Caught up in the hectic schedules of living, most people yearn for the peace Jesus can offer. And thanks to our merciful God, that peace is available to all who believe in Jesus.

 # Getting Started

Before Worship

Before the worship session, find an adult male volunteer to play the part of Zechariah in the "Surprise Visitor" activity. Provide a costume for your volunteer—a typical "Bible times" robe and beard, for example—and give your volunteer a copy of the "Zechariah's Story" script on page 33. Ask him to practice it beforehand, memorizing it if possible. Have the volunteer wait outside the room until you cue him to enter. Use pieces of poster board or paper and markers to make a cue card for each of the following words: "WOW!" "YEA!" "OOH!" "AHH!" and "UH-OH!" Set up a table for "Zechariah" to use.

Set up a TV and VCR in the elementary meeting area, and cue the *KidsOwn Worship Video* to the "The Amazing Needomatizer" segment. You'll want to watch it at least once before the session so you're familiar with it.

For the "Worship Banners" activity, you'll need a piece each of red, green, and yellow poster board. Cut the bottom of each piece to give it a banner look. (See illustration.) Provide at least three Bibles, and gather enough craft supplies for children to work in three groups. Include scissors, glue or glitter glue, and scraps of Christmas wrap or construction paper.

You'll want to darken the area used for "Let's Pray!" as much as possible, so check for ways to do that. Set up a Christmas tree in this area, or, if you can't use a real tree, cut a tree shape from green butcher paper, and tape it to a wall. Cut enough six-inch squares of Christmas wrapping paper to have at least one for each student. Set a box of ornament hooks (or tape) near the tree.

Arrival Time

Have *Songs From FaithWeaver, Vol. 6* playing as children arrive. Designate greeters to welcome children at the entrance, and ask your greeters to shake hands with them and welcome them by name.

 # Let's Praise God!

SAY Welcome, everyone! Let's take a few moments to greet each other. Turn to the people around you, and tell them you're glad they're here.

ASK • What are some reasons you came to children's church today?

SAY No matter what your reason for coming, we're all here because God brought us together, just as our first song says. Let's worship God because he meets our needs.

CD track 11 Sing "The Good Life."
Lyrics and motions are in the back of this book.

ASK • What are some ways we need God?

SAY We need God's salvation so we can live with him in heaven forever. We need God's forgiveness when we do wrong things. Sometimes, when we feel lonely or sad, we need God's love and acceptance. It's good to know that God meets our needs! God is our Father, Savior, creator, and master. Let's worship God by singing "My God Is."

Song Lyrics and Motions

To make the worship session go more smoothly, tear out the lyrics sheets in the back of the book and keep them in a separate folder. Each week, pull out only the sheets you need for the day's worship session.

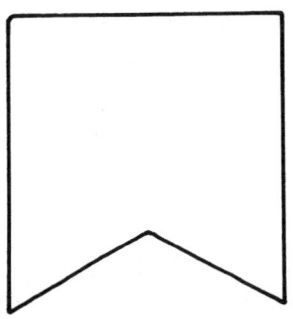

Leader SkillBuilder

It's easy for children to identify material needs—the need for food, clothing, homes, and families, for example. This lesson focuses on our *intangible* need for salvation and forgiveness. Be prepared to guide children toward thinking on a deeper level about human needs. If discussions gravitate toward physical needs, accept those responses, but prompt children to think further about those needs that we can't see, touch, smell, hear, or taste.

 Sing "My God Is."
Lyrics and motions are in the back of this book.

SAY God meets our needs. He sent Jesus to give us salvation and forgiveness, to give us hope, and to help us follow him. Let's pray, thanking God for who he is and how he meets our needs.

Invite kids to pray their own prayers of thanks aloud.

SAY God sent Jesus to meet our needs. That's exciting! Let's sing the story of how God sent Jesus.

 Sing "Mary's Boy Child."
Lyrics and motions are in the back of this book.

SAY We'll be celebrating Jesus' birth soon. That means Christmas is coming, and Christmas usually means presents, which usually bring joy! Raise your hand if you feel joy at Christmastime. Pause. Presents are fun, but God gives us something better than toys, video games, or sports equipment! God's best gift is his Son, Jesus. Jesus offers us salvation, which means he saves us from something.

ASK • What do we need to be saved from?

SAY We need to be saved from the guilt of the wrong things we do. John 3:17 says, "For God did not send his Son into the world to condemn the world, but to save the world through him." That's joyful news! Let's sing our next song joyfully, as if we're proclaiming the good news to the world.

 Sing "Joy to the World!"
Lyrics and motions are in the back of this book.

SAY In today's Bible story, God told Zechariah that God would send a Savior to meet our needs. And you know what? God kept that promise! Soon after Zechariah prophesied about him, Jesus was born.

 Sing "Just Like You Promised."
Lyrics and motions are in the back of this book.

SAY Christmastime is a joyful time. Presents, special foods, and being with family and friends all make us happy. God wants us to feel that joy at other times, too. Tell us about a time you felt joy because God met a need you had or because of something he did for you. Give children time to respond.

ASK • What are some ways we can express our joy?

After children respond, ask a few volunteers to lead the class in expressing joy by shouting, dancing, jumping up and down, or doing something else children suggested.

SAY Jesus also brings us peace. Sit down now, and show me how you look when you're peaceful. That's great! I feel more peaceful already just looking at you!

ASK • Does God's joy help meet our needs? Why?

SAY When we have God's joy, it helps us keep going, even when things are tough or when they don't turn out the way we expected. During our next song, let's smile to show our joy that God meets our needs.

 Sing "For to Us a Child Is Born" (Isaiah 9:6).
Lyrics and motions are in the back of this book.

SAY God sent Jesus to us, but are we ready for him? God wants us to get ready for Jesus by asking him to be Lord in our lives.

ASK • What does "Jesus is Lord" mean?
• How can we show Jesus that he's our Lord?

SAY Let's make Jesus Lord by making him the most important person in our lives. Make room for him in your heart, and let him be in charge of everything.

 Sing "Jesus Is Lord of All."
Lyrics and motions are in the back of this book.

SAY Jesus is Lord of everything, and he loves us. Think of some reasons to love Jesus. On the count of three, call out your reason. Ready? One, two, three! Pause. Those are great reasons! Jesus heard every one of them! Now let's tell Jesus we love him by singing the next song on our knees. We'll sing it as a prayer, showing God we want him to be Lord in our lives.

 Sing "I Love You, Lord."
Lyrics and motions are in the back of this book.

PRAY God, thank you for helping us see that we need you. Thank you for meeting our needs. Thank you for sending Jesus to give us salvation, hope, forgiveness, and help in following you. In Jesus' name, amen.

Let's Learn the Point!

PRESCHOOL ACTIVITIES, pp. 29-30

At this time, have the preschool helper invite the preschoolers to go to their own room for this section of activities. Tear out the Preschool Activities page and give it to the preschool leader. Have the preschool leader bring the preschoolers back to participate in the prayer time with the older children. If you prefer to keep all the children together, do the starred activities. They will work well with both elementary and preschool children.

ELEMENTARY ACTIVITIES

✴ Surprise Visitor

Cue your volunteer "Zechariah" that it's time to enter the meeting area.

SAY We have a surprise visitor with us today. It isn't often we get to visit with someone from the Bible! Zechariah has agreed to visit our worship session and tell us about something that happened to him. Zechariah, I understand you've had quite an experience. Please tell us about it.

Lead children in responding to the volunteer when he holds up the cue cards. When "Zechariah" is finished, thank him, and lead the children in clapping for him.

ASK • According to Zechariah, what do people need?
• Why was Zechariah praising God?
• How did he say God would meet people's needs?

(See Worship Leader Tip)

Worship Leader Tip

Talk to the volunteer beforehand about allowing time for children to ask him questions at the end. Encourage questions that will help children better understand his message.

SAY God meets our needs by giving us hope, salvation, forgiveness from sin, and help in following him. That's why we praise God!

* The Amazing Needomatizer

 Show kids "The Amazing Needomatizer" segment from the *KidsOwn Worship Video*. The video shows a girl who has built a machine that creates whatever she needs. After the video, discuss the following questions:

ASK • Would you like to have a machine like this?
• How is God like the amazing needomatizer? How is he different?

SAY God doesn't do whatever we ask—he's not a wish machine. But the Bible does promise that God will take care of our needs.

Have the children look up Philippians 4:19. Have a volunteer read the verse aloud.

ASK • What does this verse tell us about God?
• God sent Jesus to fulfill our needs. How does Jesus meet our needs?

SAY God knew people need to be saved from their sins. God sent Jesus to take care of our needs. He saves us from our sins, he comforts us, he loves us, and he guides us. Let's learn more about God's gift to us.

Worship Banners

Have kids form three groups. Designate one the salvation and forgiveness group, one the hope group, and one the help group. Give each group craft supplies, including markers and glue, and one of the pieces of poster board you prepared earlier. Make sure each group has a Bible.

Have the groups look up the following Scriptures to help them understand their needs and how God fills them through Jesus.

• Luke 1:69-71 and Acts 4:12 (the salvation and forgiveness group)

• Psalm 42:5-6a and Micah 7:7 (the hope group)

• Isaiah 41:10 and Luke 1:74-75 (the help group)

SAY Choose someone to read the verses for your group. Then discuss with your group how God meets our needs for salvation and forgiveness, hope, and help in following him.

Give groups several minutes to read and discuss the Scriptures.

ASK • How does God meet our need for salvation and forgiveness?
• How does God's hope help us?
• How does God help us?

SAY We're going to make worship banners to thank God for meeting our needs in Jesus. Use your poster-board banner and craft supplies to illustrate what your group talked about. For example, you might write, "God gives us salvation and forgiveness," then decorate your banner with words, drawings, and designs that tell or show how God meets our needs for salvation and forgiveness through Jesus.

 Play "Joy to the World!" while the kids work. When the groups are finished with their banners, hang the banners in the meeting area, and have group members explain them.

(continued on page 31)

Preschool Activities

Zechariah Prophesies About Jesus Luke 1:68-79

Worship Theme: God meets our needs.

Using Theo

Consider using Theophilus the FaithRetriever puppet today in these ways:

• Have Theo lead the preschoolers from the main worship area to the preschool room.

• Have Theo give children the affirmations in the "Blanket of Love" activity.

• See the KidsOwn Worship Kit for a puppet skit written for today's worship session.

The Shape of Love

Before class, cut large hearts from red felt and cross shapes from green felt. Each shape should be about six inches tall, although you may want to adjust the size according to the number of children in your group and the size of the fabric you'll use for the "Blanket of Love" activity. You'll want enough shapes to make a decorative pattern on the blanket. If your class is small, give children more than one shape each.

SAY A long time ago, a priest named Zechariah told everyone that the Savior was coming soon. The Savior is someone who helps us get to heaven. Zechariah didn't know the Savior's name because he wasn't born yet. But we know the Savior's name. Who is the Savior? Pause. That's right. Jesus is the Savior!

Zechariah told people the Savior would forgive them for the wrong things they do. Make a sad face if you've ever done a wrong thing. Pause. All of us have done wrong things. Jesus will forgive you. These crosses remind us of Jesus' forgiveness. Pass out green crosses to half the children.

I have more shapes to give the rest of you. Zechariah also told the people that the Savior would show them God's great love. Zechariah said the Savior would help them and give them what they need. These hearts remind us of God's love. Pass out the felt hearts to the rest of the children. Make sure each child has at least one shape.

ASK • What things do you need Jesus to help you with?

SAY God loves to meet our needs! Zechariah said that the Savior would help us follow God. We need God's help. Hold your shape up in the air if you're glad God sent Jesus to be our Savior. Pause. Wave your shape back and forth through the air if you're glad God meets our needs. Pause. Place your shape over your heart if you love Jesus. Your shape just might stick to your shirt like Jesus sticks with us! Pause.

Let's play a game now and take our shapes over to the table. We're going to make something to remind us that God meets our needs. Ready? Follow me. Lead the children around the room, Follow-the-Leader style, to the craft table.

Blanket of Love

You'll need a piece of fabric, such as an old flannel bed-sheet. Before class, spread the fabric on the table. You'll need the felt shapes from "The Shape of Love" activity, as

(continued on page 30)

(continued from page 29)

well as one or two small safety pins per shape, bottles of glitter glue, and a low-heat glue gun. Gather the children around the blanket.

ASK • Do you have a favorite blanket to sleep with?
• How do you feel when you have your special blanket? when you don't have it?

SAY God's love feels warm and soft like a blanket. It makes us feel safe and happy. The shapes you have are to remind you of something about God.

ASK • How do your shapes make you think of God's love?

SAY The cross reminds us that Jesus forgives us when we do wrong things. The hearts remind us that God loves us and helps us. Let's use our shapes to make a special blanket to remind us of God's love. It will remind us that God meets our needs.

Help children place their shapes on the fabric to form a pattern. Then attach each shape to the blanket with one or two safety pins. Explain that the pins will hold the shapes in place until you glue them on later. When the pieces are pinned, hold the blanket up to show the children.

SAY What a special blanket to remind us of God's love! The hearts and crosses make a pretty pattern and remind us that God meets our needs. Let's take turns wrapping ourselves in the blanket—it'll feel like getting a hug from God.

Wrap each child in the blanket and say something loving to the child, such as, "Jesus loves you," or "You're special to God." Make sure everyone gets "hugged" in the blanket and affirmed. Then spread the blanket on the table again.

SAY Let's add some finishing touches to our blanket. We'll put little dots of glitter glue on our shapes to make it look extra special, like God's love. As you add dots, let's tell ways that God shows his love for us.

Help children make small dots on the felt shapes. Encourage every child to name at least one way God shows his love by meeting our needs.

Preschool Leader Tip

Use the blanket in future lessons to express God's love. For example, each child could have a turn holding it or wrapping up in it during the Bible story or playtime. Say something like, "God's love hugs us like a warm blanket."

SAY This blanket looks beautiful! Let's hang our blanket in the classroom to remind us that God meets our needs.

After class, remove the safety pins, and use the glue gun to glue the shapes to the blanket. Display the blanket in a prominent place in the classroom.

✱ Full Hearts

You'll need heart-shaped cookies, at least one per child, as well as frosting; plastic knives; napkins; and decorations, such as sprinkles and mini-candies.

ASK • How does God show his love to us?
• How can you show your love to God?

SAY God shows us his love in lots of ways. God meets our needs. God forgives us, God helps us get to heaven, and God helps us follow Jesus. God's love makes our hearts feel full and happy! Let's make our heart-shaped cookies look full and happy too. Each time we put a new decoration on, let's thank God for meeting our needs. I'll start. Thank you, God, for sending Jesus to us. Help children spread frosting and add decorations, one at a time. Encourage each child to say at least one thank-you prayer as he or she decorates. Continue until the cookies are full of decorations.

Our cookies are full of yummy things! Now it's time to make our tummies full and happy! While we eat our cookies, let's remember that God meets our needs.

(continued from page 28)

Have everyone stand under the Salvation banner. Encourage kids to call out praises to God for providing salvation. Then move everyone to the Hope and Help banners, and repeat the praise activity.

PRAY Dear God, thanks for seeing our needs and meeting them. Without you, we would be lost, hopeless, and helpless. But with you, we have salvation, forgiveness, hope, and help in following you. Thanks, Lord! In Jesus' name, amen.

Keep the banners on the wall throughout the Christmas season.

 # Let's Pray!

The Offering

SAY One way to thank God for meeting our needs is to let him use us to meet the needs of others. We should look for ways to care for others as God cares for us. Give each person a small envelope and a pencil.

ASK • Why does God want to use us to meet needs?
• How can we help meet the needs of others?
• How does giving our offerings show God we're thankful that he meets our needs?

SAY On your envelope, list specific ways God has met your needs, or draw a picture of how God takes care of you. Then, if you brought an offering, place it in the envelope and seal it. As you put your envelopes in the bowl, thank God for meeting your needs.

Pass the offering bowl, and have children put their envelopes in it.

Lord, Help Us See

Darken the room as much as possible, and light a candle.

SAY This candle is to remind us of God's presence. God is with us all the time, and he meets our needs.

Have children find a place in the room to sit or stand quietly with eyes closed.

SAY Let's ask God to show us some needs to pray for. They might be our needs or the needs of others—needs for salvation and forgiveness, hope, or help in following him. I'm going to pray first, then you repeat after me. Remember, God listens when we talk to him!

PRAY God, we come to you right now. Pause while children repeat. We are listening for you. Pause. Speak to each of us in our hearts. Pause. Show us needs that we can pray for. Pause. Thank you, God. Pause. In Jesus' name, amen.

SAY Keep your eyes closed now and be totally quiet for several more seconds. Think about the needs that come to your mind. Pause for about thirty seconds before continuing.

The things that came to your mind are needs that you can ask God to meet. Let's get ready to pray for those needs in a fun way.

Worship Leader Tip

It may be helpful to walk around the room during this activity to help kids stay quiet and focused on God. If a child is having difficulty being quiet, gently touch her on the shoulder and whisper a reminder to focus on God during this time.

Christmas Prayer Tree

Have children form small groups. Give each group squares of Christmas wrapping paper, scissors, and pencils or markers.

SAY To make a Christmas ornament, cut the piece of wrapping paper in any shape you want. On the back of your ornament, write the needs that came to your mind when we prayed a few minutes ago. When you're finished writing, come get an ornament hook and hang your ornament on the tree. Our Christmas tree is a way of offering our prayers to God.

track 2 Play "Just Like You Promised" as children work. Allow children to make more than one ornament if time permits. When everyone has hung an ornament, gather around the tree.

SAY God has seen the things you've written on your ornaments. He hears our prayers and meets our needs. That gives us hope! Let's pray.

PRAY Lord, we put these needs on our Christmas tree for you to see. Thank you for knowing and understanding each of them. You understand even the things that aren't written down. Thank you, God, for loving us and meeting every need we have. In Jesus' name, amen.

Why We Worship

We worship a powerful God who is righteous and just. He rules over heaven and earth, yet he has time to be concerned with individuals. Based on his knowledge of the intricacies of our nature, and on the holiness of his nature, God has pointed out attitudes and behaviors he wants to see in us. These attitudes and behaviors are the same for all of us, even though they may look different for each of us. We stand in wonder that God's plans are so global—yet so personal. The God who set the earth in its orbit cares about how *I* act today. We try to live right to honor his great and caring plans for us and those around us.

Bible Background

Luke 3:7-18

We often hear of John the Baptist's mission: "A voice of one calling in the desert, 'Prepare the way for the Lord, make straight paths for him'" (Luke 3:4b-6). However, we don't often hear much about John's message.

From his name, most people understand that John baptized people. Crowds came to him to be baptized as a symbol of being cleansed of their former way of life and as a commitment to worship the true God of Israel. However, Luke 3:7-18 makes it clear that John didn't willingly baptize and bless everyone who came to him.

John's strong admonition in Luke 3:7 was directed at those whose requests to be baptized stemmed from a desire to satisfy outward appearances rather than a sincere intention to change their unfaithful ways. John was demanding changed lives as a visible sign that people had turned to God.

John pointed out that those who believed they had an advantage because they were descendants of Abraham were mistaken. Who their ancestors were was unimportant. What counted was repentance. John wanted people to truly repent and turn to God because he saw the judgment coming. God was about to get rid of the unfruitful trees. John knew that judgment was about to come to the Jews, and it did forty years later when Jerusalem was destroyed.

It should be made clear that John's statements in Luke 3:10-14 are not requirements for salvation. They are examples of what John was suggesting—lives that are changed as a result of choosing to live for God.

Crowds of people thronged to hear John and be baptized; many accepted his cutting message; some even suggested that he himself might be the Messiah (Luke 3: 15). In the face of such acclamation, John could easily have allowed himself to become a prideful leader. However, his statement in Luke 3:16 reveals his true character. He was fully aware of the greatness of the One who was yet to begin his ministry, One for whom he felt unworthy of performing the most humble task—untying his sandals.

Skits and Puppets

In the KidsOwn Worship Kit, you'll find a collection of skits titled, "KidsOwn Worship Skits." The skits are designed to be used with Theophilus the FaithRetriever puppet during the preschool activities. You can purchase a Theo puppet at your local Christian bookstore.

Song Lyrics and Motions

To make the worship session go more smoothly, tear out the lyrics sheets from the back of this book and keep them in a separate folder. Each week, pull out only the sheets you need for the day's worship session.

Getting Started

Before Worship

Before the worship session, stuff junk mail, newsprint, and other trash in a gift box. Make photocopies of the handout on page 44, and prepare the bags for "It's in the Bag."

 Set up a TV and VCR. Cue the *KidsOwn Worship Video* to the segment titled "A Family Outing." You'll want to watch the segment at least once before the children arrive so you're familiar with the video.

For the "Making Room for Jesus" activity, prepare a lunch bag for each child by crumpling a piece of paper and putting the crumpled paper in the lunch bag.

Arrival Time

Have *Songs From FaithWeaver, Vol. 6* playing as children arrive. Greet each child by name, and say, "Jesus is coming! Are you ready?" Have children tell other children how they are preparing for Jesus to come.

Let's Praise God!

SAY Hello, everyone! We are here to worship and honor God!

ASK • What does it mean to honor God?

SAY Coming to church is one way to honor God—and you've all done that today—but we also honor him by living right all week long. Greet your neighbor with a handshake or a high-five right now. Then tell your neighbor something you did this week that honored God.

ASK • Why would we want to live lives that honor God?

SAY We serve an awesome God who created tall mountains and mighty rivers. God also created each of you and cares enough about you to count the hairs on your head. God sent his one and only Son to live in our world and to pay the price for our sins. And God's preparing a special home for each of you in heaven.

ASK • Why do you think God has done all this for you?

SAY You must really matter to God. God loves you and cares about what happens to each one of you. That gives me joy and makes me want to live in a way that shows that God matters to me! I want to show my love and gratitude to him. Let's stand and sing "Joy to the World!" to celebrate the gift of Jesus, our king.

 Sing "Joy to the World!"
Lyrics and motions are in the back of this book.

ASK • What do you think "Let every heart prepare him room" means?

SAY Let's think about getting ready for Jesus as we sing a song that tells the Christmas story and reminds us of our Christmas present from God. Let's sing about Christmas.

Worship Leader Tip

Treat today's subject matter carefully. Be sure children understand that, while living according to God's rules honors him, it won't save them. You may want to take the time today to carefully explain to children that we are saved through our faith in Jesus rather than through good deeds. We don't follow God's rules in order to earn his favor—we already have his unconditional love. As Christians, we live according to God's rules because Jesus has set us free from sin. And we live according to God's rules because we want to show him our love, our devotion, and our commitment.

 **track 3**
Sing "Mary's Boy Child."
Lyrics and motions are in the back of this book.

 **track 21**
Sing "For to Us a Child Is Born."
Lyrics and motions are in the back of this book.

ASK • **How does it make you feel to think about Jesus leaving heaven and coming to earth to show his love?**

SAY **Jesus' coming to earth brought us joy, love, and light from the heart of God. It's good to think about and praise God for those gifts that Jesus brought to us. Let's sing, "Joy!" as we honor God for sending Jesus to be our king.**

 **track 5**
Sing "Joy!"
Lyrics and motions are in the back of this book.

SAY **Joy, love, and light are wonderful gifts that God gave when he sent his Son, Jesus. We talked earlier about the meaning of "prepare him room," but we didn't really talk about** *how* **to do that. Let's say I want to give a gift.** Show the gift you brought, and tell who it's for. **I have a box to put it in.** Show the box. Ask one of the children to help you by opening the box.

What's all this! Name some of the things you've stuffed in the box while you pull them out and put them back in the box. Then try to put the gift inside the box. The lid shouldn't fit well with everything inside the box. Ponder aloud how the person you're giving the gift to might feel about receiving all your trash along with the gift.

ASK • **What do you think I should do?**

Remove all the trash from the box, and line it with clean tissue paper.

SAY **Now the box is prepared for the gift I have to give.** Place the gift in the box, cover it with the tissue, and put the lid on.

ASK • **How is the box like our hearts?**
• **How can our hearts be cleaned out?**

SAY **God wants our hearts to be clean so that he can fill us with the gift of his Son. After the sin is cleaned out of our lives, we can begin to live right. Living right is like lining the box with fresh tissue paper. It tells God we believe that he deserves more than our trash. As we sing our next song, think about how important Jesus is.**

 **track 10**
Sing "We Believe in God."
Lyrics and motions are in the back of this book.

SAY **I brought something fun to show you today.**

Hold up the yo-yo.

SAY **This is my new yo-yo. I've never tried it, but the package says it can do all sorts of cool tricks. Isn't it a pretty color?**

Describe the yo-yo, and explain that it can do Walk the Dog, Around the World, Rock the Cradle, Around the Corner, and other cool tricks.

SAY **A yo-yo like this can do incredible tricks. Let's test it.**

Release the yo-yo so that it goes down and stays down. Frown. Roll it up and try again. Look perplexed.

Leader SkillBuilder

Object lessons can be seen as mini-performances. Some, like this one, require rehearsal. Read the yo-yo segment carefully, and practice it two or three times. As you practice, try to anticipate and prepare for the children's responses. Watch for possible problems, and fix them before children's church. If the yo-yo works, you won't make your point.

SAY This isn't a good yo-yo. It didn't do anything!

ASK • Why do you think my yo-yo didn't work?

Let the children share their ideas.

SAY Maybe it wasn't the yo-yo's fault. Maybe I just haven't learned how to use the yo-yo right.

Ask if anyone else would like to try the yo-yo. Let several volunteers test the yo-yo.

<table>
<tr><td>

Worship Leader Tip

If you have a large class, provide several yo-yos. Let every interested child have a turn.

</td></tr>
</table>

SAY I guess you've proven there's nothing wrong with this yo-yo. It's built perfectly to do what it's supposed to do. But the person using the yo-yo has to use it the right way to make it do great things. We're made to honor God. But if we don't live right—if we don't use our lives the way God made them to be used—God can't be honored.

One of the most important parts of living right is loving with the love of Jesus. God is honored when we act as Jesus acted. Let's sing the song "Love With the Love of Jesus."

 Sing "Love With the Love of Jesus." Lyrics and motions are in the back of this book.

SAY God promised to send his Son to save his people from their sins. That promise is for us, too. Jesus came to give us clean hearts, to fill us with the good gifts of God, and to give us a good life.

 Sing "The Good Life." Lyrics and motions are in the back of this book.

PRAY Lord, we thank you for coming. We welcome you to our lives. Thank you for giving us the good life. Help us live right and honor you in everything we do. In Jesus' name, amen.

Let's Learn the Point!

PRESCHOOL ACTIVITIES, pp. 39-40

At this time, have the preschool helper invite the preschoolers to go to their own room for this section of activities. Tear out the Preschool Activities page, and give it to the preschool leader. Have the preschool leader bring the preschoolers back to participate in the prayer time with the older children. If you prefer to keep all the children together, do the starred activities. They will work well with both elementary and preschool children.

ELEMENTARY ACTIVITIES

✳ "A Family Outing"

 Show the video segment titled "A Family Outing" about a family on a special outing. Distracted by games they're playing in the car, the kids miss the parent's announcement about a neat exhibit.

(continued on page 41)

Preschool Activities 3

John Prepares People for Jesus' Coming Luke 3:7-18
Worship Theme: Living right honors God.

Using Theo

Consider using Theophilus today in these ways:

• Have Theo lead the preschoolers from the main worship area to the preschool room.

• Have Theo lead the song, "Jesus Christ Is Coming to Town."

• See the KidsOwn Worship Kit for a puppet skit written for today's worship session.

Jesus Christ Is Coming to Town

Gather the children in a circle.

SAY Raise your hand if you know the song, "Santa Claus Is Coming to Town." Pause to allow children to raise their hands. **That song teaches us we need to be good so we'll get a lot of presents.**

ASK • Do you think getting presents is a reason to be good? Why, or why not?
• Are there other, better reasons for being good?

SAY We try to be good because we love Jesus and want to honor God. Today we're going to sing that song in a way that will honor God. We'll call the song, "Jesus Christ Is Coming to Town," because it will soon be Christmas.

Sing this song one line at a time, and have the children repeat each line after you.

Jesus Christ Is Coming to Town

Oh, prepare your hearts well.	*(Place your hands over your heart.)*

Live for Jesus and pray,	*(Shade your eyes with one hand as if looking far away, then fold your hands for prayer.)*
Obey your parents	*(Point your right index finger twice.)*
Every day.	*(Open your arms wide.)*
Jesus Christ is coming to town.	*(Point up.)*
Oh, prepare your hearts well.	*(Place your hands over your heart.)*
Live for Jesus and pray,	*(Shade your eyes with one hand as if looking far away, then fold your hands for prayer.)*
Obey your parents	*(Point your right index finger twice.)*
Every day.	*(Open your arms wide.)*
Jesus Christ is coming to town.	*(Point up.)*
He watches while you're sleeping.	*(Shade your eyes, then rest your head on your hands as if on a pillow.)*
He sees you when you sing.	*(Sing "la-la.")*
He loves and wants to be your friend,	*(Hug yourself.)*
And we honor him as king!	*(Point up, then point right index finger twice.)*

(Repeat chorus.)

SAY The Bible tells us about a man who was sent by God to help people get ready for Jesus. His name was John the Baptist. He told people that they should live right to show they were sorry for the bad things they'd done. If John had been talking to kids like you, he might have said something like this:

Repeat the song, along with the motions.

ASK • Why do you think John told people to live right?

SAY Living right honors God.

(continued on page 40)

(continued from page 39)

ASK • How can we live to honor God?

SAY God is so pleased when we love, obey, and live right. That's how we prepare our hearts for Jesus. Let's sing our new song together once more. Sing the song one more time.

✳ It's in the Bag

Before the session, prepare one set of bags for every three children. In each set, one bag should contain three bears cut from the handout (p. 44), one bag should contain three coats cut from the same handout, and one bag should contain a glue stick.

Help the children form groups of three and find places to sit in their groups. Give each child in the group a bag, but tell children to wait to open the bags.

SAY These paper bags will help us learn a lesson about living right. Follow my directions. I want each of you to put a coat on a teddy bear by using what's in your bag. Now open your own bag, and look at what's inside. Don't tell your friends what it is.

ASK • Can you use what's in your bag to put a coat on a teddy bear?

SAY Hmm. It seems that you each have a problem. Tell the others in your group what your problem is. Walk around and help any children who are having difficulty expressing themselves to their partners.

ASK • Can any of your groups come up with a way to fix the problems you are all having?

SAY The idea you came up with is the same one that John the Baptist taught people. He told them to share. He said that sharing was part of living right. You can share right now so that each of you can have a teddy bear wearing a coat. If you have bears, give one to everyone in your group including yourself. If you have coats, give a coat to everyone. If you have the glue stick, share it in your group. As you share, say "I share to honor God." Let the kids complete the task on their own. Walk around to give individual instruction to any group having difficulty, and to remind the children that living right honors God. When everyone is finished, collect the bears, and gather the children in a circle.

I saw lots of things in your group that honor God. I saw sharing, cooperating, kindness, and helpfulness.

Mention any other good things you saw. **You are learning to live right, and that honors God. Let's play a game next.**

✳ Spotlight on Good Deeds

Have the children stand in a circle. Choose one child to stand in the middle of the circle, and give that child a flashlight.

SAY Living right honors God. That means when we do the things we are supposed to do, we show God how much we love and respect him. We shouldn't act right just at Christmas time so we can get presents. We should do right things because God is great and powerful, and we want to honor him.

We're going to play a game to learn more about living right to honor God. I'm going to turn out the lights and play some music. While the music is playing, [name of child in the middle] will walk around the circle and shine the flashlight on different children's feet. When the music stops, our friend will stop moving the light. Whoever's feet are in the light will tell something we can do to show our love for God.

Turn out the lights, and play a CD or tape of children's music. Stop the music whenever you wish. Have the child caught in the light name an action that would honor God. Let this child move to the middle to shine the flashlight for the next round of the game. Play several times.

Have children stay in a circle and hold hands.

SAY You came up with some great ideas! When we do those things, we are living right, and living right honors our (lead the children in bending down so that your hands almost touch the floor) **great,** (lead the children in holding their hands out in front of their knees) **mighty,** (continue, lifting your hands to waist level) **holy,** (raise your hands to shoulder level) **loving,** (raise your hands above your head, and wave them) **God! Shake your arms to praise him together!**

> **Preschool Leader Tip**
>
> Have crayons or markers ready to give to groups who finish the task quickly. Suggest that they decorate the bears' coats.

> **Preschool Leader Tip**
>
> For safety's sake, and because some children th[is] age are afraid of the dark, don't turn the lights off completely. Leave a door o[r] window open a bit, or dim the lights, if possible. The room should be just dark enough to make the light from the flashlight visible. Also insist that the children shine the light at feet and not into faces.

(continued from page 38)

After the video, ask the following questions:

ASK • Has anything like this ever happened to you?
• How do you think the kids felt about missing out on something so cool?
• How do you think the parents felt when the kids missed out?
• What did these kids do wrong?
• What do you think the kids wished they had done differently?

SAY Let's suppose that we're in a situation similar to the one we saw in the video. Let's suppose that Jesus is coming—and we're the only ones who know it. The rest of the world is busy going about its business. We want to make sure people don't miss out on seeing Jesus. Find a partner, and come up with a plan to spread the news about Jesus. Think about how you're going to persuade people to pay attention to your message. Think about how you're going to get people to get ready for Jesus.

Give the children two minutes to come up with a plan. Then have each pair find another pair to make a foursome. Have kids in each pair explain their plan to the other pair in the foursome.

ASK • Why is it so important that people realize who Jesus is?
• How do you think John the Baptist felt when he was spreading the word about who Jesus is?
• How do you think he felt about people who listened to his message?
• How do you think he felt when some people didn't pay any attention to his message?

SAY I think the kids in the video felt awful about missing out during their trip. I know for sure that people who miss out on Jesus will be terribly disappointed when they realize how great Jesus is. John the Baptist had a very important message to tell. He wanted people to know that Jesus was the best thing that had ever happened. And he had a specific plan to help people get ready for Jesus so they wouldn't miss out on him. Let's learn more about John the Baptist's plan.

Room for God

Gather the children around the large box.

SAY Let's see if there's room for all of you in this box.

Let the children try to squeeze into the box.

SAY You tried really hard to fit everyone in the box, but there just wasn't room for all of you.

ASK • How do you feel now that you realize you can't all fit?
• How did you feel if you were left out of the box?
• Can you think of anything else you might do to fit everyone in?

If there were observers for this activity, let them tell what they saw and offer any suggestions that might have occurred to them. Let kids try their ideas, then sit down together.

SAY John the Baptist told people what they needed to do to get ready for Jesus. John told the people that their lives were kind of like our box as we tried to get everyone in it. John said their lives were crowded with sinful, selfish things. He told people to show that they were really sorry for their sins and to start doing the right thing. Let's explore what John told the people.

Worship Leader Tip

Some of the children may prefer to sit this game out. They may be claustrophobic, shy, or even too dressed up. Let those who prefer to sit out serve as observers. Have them record and share their observations with the rest of the class.

Have children form small groups, and have each group look up Luke 3:3-16. Have the groups read the passage and answer the following questions.

ASK • **What was John the Baptist's job? Look at verses 3-4.**
• **What did John tell the people to do to get ready for Jesus? Look at verses 10-14.**
• **Why do you think John gave them the instructions he did? Look at verses 15-16.**
• **How will following John's instructions help these people get ready for Jesus?**

Have the groups report their findings.

SAY **John said that, to get ready for Jesus, we need to be sorry for our sins and honor God by living right. John wanted the people to uncrowd their lives by getting rid of things or not doing things that were wrong or that took their focus from God. Now let's look at how we can prepare for Jesus.**

Making Room for Jesus

SAY **John the Baptist told people to stop doing wrong things and to start doing good things. He wanted people to see that doing only what they wanted to do takes up all the space in their hearts—it doesn't leave any room for Jesus.**

Let's pretend that Jesus is coming and that we're getting ready for him, just as the people in the Bible were doing. Think about what things you'd like to take out of your life to make room for Jesus. Also think about the things you'd like to add to your life to show that you're living for Jesus.

Hand out the paper lunch bags you prepared before worship. Also hand out pencils and index cards. Have the children take the crumpled paper out of the paper bag, smooth it, and list on it the things they'd like to take out of their lives. Have the children list on the index cards the things they'd like to add to their lives. Have them put the index cards inside the paper bags and put the bags under the Christmas tree.

SAY **John wanted the people to pay attention to the things they did. He wanted them to make good choices about their actions. John knew that, when the people started living right, they'd be ready to welcome Jesus. And John knew that right living would please and honor God.**

PRAY **God, we know that it's important to get ready for Jesus. We want to get ready for Jesus by living our lives in a way that's pleasing to you. Please help us live for you every day.**

 Let's Pray!

The Offering

SAY Giving an offering is like giving an extra tunic to someone who doesn't have one. It's being so happy with what we have that we are willing to share with others. Maybe you didn't bring money today, but you'd still like to honor God with generosity. While we take the offering, tell God about a way that you will live "rightly," a way you can be more generous, or a way you can be more fair.

PRAY Lord, we honor you today. We give offerings because it's the right thing to do. We want to show you are our God by doing the right thing. We want to live right to honor you. In Jesus' name, amen. Take the offering.

Prayer of Confession

Give each child a slip of paper and a pencil.

SAY Anything that keeps us from living right is sin. But I have good news from 1 John 1:9: "If we confess our sins, he is faithful and just and will forgive us our sins and purify us from all unrighteousness." That means, if we tell God about the wrong things we do, he will forgive us and help us to live right.

Let's make that verse really personal for each of us. Let's substitute a blank as we read it. We'll say, "If I confess *blank*...he is faithful and just and will forgive *blank*...and purify me from all unrighteousness."

Now write or draw on your paper a picture of whatever you filled in the blank with in your mind. No one is going to look. Only God will know what you write. When you finish, crumple your paper into a little ball.

Give the children time to do this.

SAY I have a trash can up here. After you've asked God to forgive you, come put your paper in the trash.

Let the children do this and return to their seats.

SAY Let's use 1 John 1:9 as a prayer.

Have the children repeat the following after you, a phrase at a time.

PRAY Lord, we confess our sins. You are faithful and just. You will forgive our sins. You purify us. May we live right and honor you. In Jesus' name, amen.

He Is Really God

SAY Let's celebrate! This song will be a prayer of praise for the power Jesus has to help us live right and honor God.

 Sing "He Is Really God."
Lyrics and motions are in the back of this book.

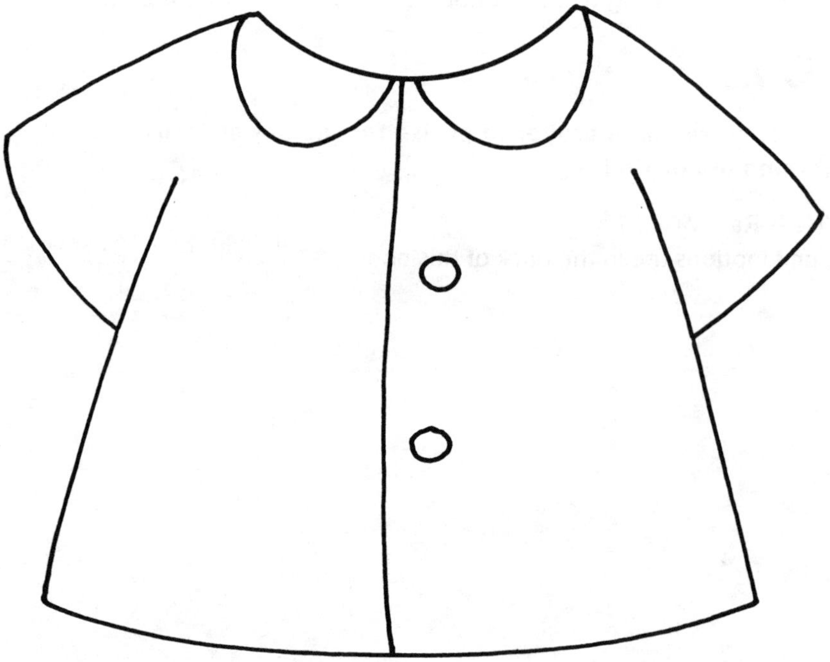

The Son of God Is Born!

Luke 1:26-45; 2:1-20

Worship Theme: Jesus' birth is something to celebrate.

A Look at the Session

Session Sequence	What Children Will Do	Supplies
Getting Started	Find a warm welcome at children's church.	**KidsOwn Worship Kit:** *Songs From FaithWeaver, Vol. 6* **Classroom Supplies:** CD player, candy canes
Let's Praise God! 1 (up to 25 minutes)	**Sing:** • "Just Like You Promised" (track 2) • "Mary's Boy Child" (track 3) • "Joy to the World!" (track 1) • "Joy!" (track 5) • "He Is Really God" (track 8) • "Your Everlasting Love" (track 17) • "For to Us a Child Is Born" (Isaiah 9:6) (track 21)	**KidsOwn Worship Kit:** *Songs From FaithWeaver, Vol. 6;* Lyrics Transparencies **Classroom Supplies:** CD player, overhead projector, large box with lid, wrapping paper, bow, Christmas tree with lights, candy canes

2 Let's Learn the Point! — PRESCHOOL ACTIVITIES (up to 25 minutes)

What Children Will Do	Supplies
Story Ornaments—Decorate Christmas ornaments to tell the story of Jesus' birth.	**Classroom Supplies:** Red felt, scissors, glitter glue, Christmas stickers, yellow yarn, cotton balls, glue
✳ **Birthday Celebration**—Throw a birthday party for Jesus.	**Classroom Supplies:** Decorations, tape, paper plates, cups, napkins, drinks, frosted cupcakes, sprinkles or candies
Musical Cheers—Play a game to clap and cheer for Jesus' birth.	**Classroom Supplies:** Jingle bells, twist-ties, cassette or CD player, Christmas cassette or CD

2 Let's Learn the Point! — ELEMENTARY ACTIVITIES (up to 25 minutes)

What Children Will Do	Supplies
✳ **A Joyful Noise**—Watch the Bible story on video and celebrate with it.	**KidsOwn Worship Kit:** *KidsOwn Worship Video:* "This Little Child" **Classroom Supplies:** TV, VCR, Bibles, noisemakers
Presents for Jesus—Discuss what Jesus wants for his birthday, and prepare gifts to give him.	**KidsOwn Worship Kit:** *Songs From FaithWeaver, Vol. 6:* "Just Like You Promised" (track 2) **Classroom Supplies:** CD player, index cards, markers, colored pencils
✳ **Christmas Story Luminarias**—Make luminarias that illustrate the story of Jesus' birth.	**Classroom Supplies:** Small paper sacks, sand, bucket, measuring cup, craft supplies, glue, votive candles

Session Sequence	What Children Will Do	Supplies
Let's Pray! 3 (up to 10 minutes)	**The Offering**—Place gifts and offerings to Jesus in a large gift-wrapped box.	**KidsOwn Worship Kit:** *Songs From FaithWeaver, Vol. 6:* "Joy to the World!" (track 1) **Classroom Supplies:** CD player, gift-wrapped box from Let's Praise God, cards from "Presents for Jesus," blank cards
	Celebration Cheers—Think of cheers of praise to God, celebrating Jesus' birth.	
	Celebration Prayers—Thank God for the gifts he has given them.	

✳ Starred activities can be used successfully with preschool and elementary children together.

Customize your session to fit your needs. You can separate preschoolers and elementary children for Section 2.

Or, if you keep the children all together for the entire worship session, we suggest you choose from the starred activities.

Why We Worship

The mighty, miraculous, mysterious power of God was displayed in the birth of Jesus, who came to earth, fully God and yet fully human, as a helpless newborn baby. The world was in desperate need of the salvation, hope, and light that Jesus brought. Some people understood their need and received Jesus with open arms, while others continued to grope in darkness.

When we recognize our spiritual needs, Jesus' love can fill our lives. He paid the price for our sins. He gives us hope in a hopeless world. And he shows us the way to a relationship with God. Let's worship God by celebrating the birth of the One who made all these things possible!

Skits and Puppets

In the KidsOwn Worship Kit, you'll find a collection of skits titled, "KidsOwn Worship Skits." The skits are designed to be used with Theophilus the FaithRetriever puppet during the preschool activities. You can purchase a Theo puppet at your local Christian bookstore.

Bible Background

Luke 1:26-45; 2:1-20

Mary and Joseph's betrothal was quite different from engagements today. In fact, in Jewish culture at that time, a betrothed couple had already taken public vows and was legally bound as in a marriage, except that the couple was not to live together or have intercourse until the appointed time. Furthermore, it is made clear in Luke 1:27 and 34 that Mary was indeed a virgin.

Mary was troubled at the angel's greeting, probably because she was confused. She might have been asking herself how she could be so highly favored by God when her family was a lowly one in Israel. But her confusion only intensified when the angel went on to explain what was to come!

Mary's initial response to the angel (Luke 1:34) doesn't indicate any hesitation in wanting the angel's message to be true. To be the mother of the Messiah was the dream of every Jewish woman. However, Mary had not yet lived with Joseph, and she knew the humiliation she would experience if it became known that she was pregnant. She also questioned the physical possibility of such a pregnancy.

When Mary was told how the child would be conceived and was reminded that God can do anything, she responded in humble obedience. She was God's servant, and she wanted God's plan to be fulfilled in her life.

We don't know if Mary went alone to visit Elizabeth, but it seems she left in a hurry, though the trip must have taken five days. Elizabeth's proclamation that Mary would bear the child of God was a final confirmation to Mary of all that she had likely been thinking during those five days of travel. With that realization, Mary burst into the poem we know as the Magnificat, as she gave glory to God for sending Jesus to earth through her.

 # Getting Started

Before Worship

Wrap a large box and its lid in Christmas wrapping paper, and put a bow on the lid. Make sure you can open the box without unwrapping it.

 Set up a TV and a VCR in the room where your elementary children will be meeting. Cue the *KidsOwn Worship Video* to the segment titled "This Little Child," and watch it at least once so you'll be familiar with it.

Arrival Time

Have *Songs From FaithWeaver, Vol. 6* playing as children arrive. Greet children by name, and give each one a candy cane as he or she enters the worship area. Tell the children not to eat the candy canes.

 # Let's Praise God!

SAY **Welcome, everyone! There's excitement in the air today! Could it be because it's almost Christmas? Let's celebrate the birth of Jesus!**

Ask volunteers to come to the front of the room and tell how their families celebrate Christmas.

SAY **The last few weeks we've been talking about God's promise to send Jesus. God kept his promise! Jesus' birth is something to celebrate.**

 Sing "Just Like You Promised."
Lyrics and motions are in the back of this book.

SAY **Now, quickly greet your neighbor, and tell your neighbor about the best Christmas gift you ever got.**

Point out the large gift-wrapped box with a bow on it.

SAY **God gave us the best Christmas gift of all. If that gift were in this box, what would be in the box? Jesus would be in it! Let's say his name together. "Jesus!" Louder! "Jesus!" That's great! We'll use this box later to prepare a gift for Jesus. Our next song is about the best gift of all.**

 Sing "Mary's Boy Child."
Lyrics and motions are in the back of this book.

SAY **Jesus really is the best gift ever. He brings joy to the world.** Lead children in singing "Joy to the World!"

 Sing "Joy to the World!"
Lyrics and motions are in the back of this book.

SAY **Let's celebrate Jesus' birth. Let's clap and cheer, jump around, dance, and show our joy in whatever way we want. Let's show God that we have joy because Jesus was born!**

Song Lyrics and Motions

To make the worship session go more smoothly, tear out the lyrics sheets at the back of this book and keep them in a separate folder. Each week, pull out only the sheets you need for the day's worship session.

Leader SkillBuilder

Children will be excited about Christmas and easily distracted during this Christmas Eve session. Use these activities to channel their energy into positive expressions of their excitement. For example, if you notice an extra measure of fidgeting during discussions and activities, take a brief "Praise and Wiggle" break. Have children stand and wiggle their whole bodies as they say "Thank you, God, for Christmas!" or something similar. Then have them sit again. If their focus begins to drift to the more commercial aspects of Christmas, be patient, but gently draw the focus back to celebrating the birth of Jesus.

 Sing "Joy!"
Lyrics and motions are in the back of this book.

Help the children form three groups based on where they're sitting.

SAY **When I point to your group, I want you to stand, shout out the praise I'm going to assign you, then quickly sit down again. Group one, you'll shout, "Jesus is born!" Group two, you'll shout, "Celebrate Jesus!" Group three, you'll shout, "Jesus is God!"**

Have groups practice their parts once, then point to the groups at random, and have them shout their parts. Have them say their praise words fast, then slow, then loud, and then soft. End by having all the groups whisper their praise at the same time.

SAY **That was great! Now let's use our enthusiasm to sing about how Jesus came to earth to help us. He is really God!**

 Sing "He Is Really God."
Lyrics and motions are in the back of this book.

Point out the Christmas tree displayed in the room.

SAY **When you came to class today, you were given a candy cane. Take your candy cane, and hold it upside down.**

ASK • **What do you see?**

SAY **The candy cane forms a J, which stands for Jesus! You can keep your candy cane for yourself. If you want to praise Jesus now for coming to earth, come and get another candy cane. Then say something like, "I praise you, Jesus, for loving me," and hang your candy cane on the tree. Let's see if we can fill our tree with praises!**

Give candy canes to children who come forward, and encourage them to praise Jesus aloud before hanging their canes on the tree.

SAY **The tree looks great! Have you ever noticed that trees always seem to point up and reach their branches out? Jesus' love is like that, it reaches higher than the sky and out to us. That's what our next song says. Let's go back to our seats and sing "Your Everlasting Love."**

 Sing "Your Everlasting Love."
Lyrics and motions are in the back of this book.

SAY **Isaiah 9:6 talks about Jesus coming to earth as a baby. It says, "For to us a child is born, to us a son is given, and the government will be on his shoulders. And he will be called Wonderful Counselor, Mighty God, Everlasting Father, Prince of Peace." God gave Jesus to us, and that's an amazing gift. Let's sing!**

 Sing "For to Us a Child Is Born" (Isaiah 9:6).
Lyrics and motions are in the back of this book.

PRAY **Dear God, thank you so much for sending Jesus to be born as a baby and to be our Savior. Help us to appreciate your gift and truly celebrate Jesus this Christmas. In Jesus' name, amen.**

Let's Learn the Point!

ELEMENTARY ACTIVITIES

✱ A Joyful Noise

SAY Let's watch a video that shows us why Jesus' birth is something to celebrate. As you watch the video, you may want to follow along in your Bibles in Luke 2:1-20. Show kids the video segment titled "This Little Child" from the *KidsOwn Worship Video.*

Give each person a noisemaker, such as a party favor or a kazoo.

SAY Now let's watch the video again. Every time you see something in the video to celebrate, use your noisemaker! Show the video segment again. When the segment is over, ask kids to set their noisemakers on the floor at their feet or put them in their pockets.

ASK • How do we know Jesus is God's Son?
• Why is Jesus' birth something to celebrate?
• How can we celebrate Jesus' birth?

SAY Jesus' birth is something to celebrate because he was the answer to God's promise. Hundreds and thousands of people, throughout all generations since Adam and Eve, had waited for Jesus to come to show us the way back to God. He kept his promise and sent Jesus to earth. That's reason to celebrate!

Encourage children to take their noisemakers home and use them to celebrate Jesus' birth on Christmas day.

Presents for Jesus

SAY When it's your birthday, what's the main thing you look forward to? Probably presents! Let's treat Jesus to some presents today for his birthday.

ASK • Does Jesus need toys or clothes? Food or games?

SAY No. Jesus has everything he needs. After all, he owns everything in the universe! But there is something he wants that only you can give him.

ASK • What would that be? What does Jesus want more than anything?

SAY Our love is the only thing he doesn't have if we don't give it to him. Our love is what he wants! He wants *you* for a friend. Think about it this way.

ASK • How do your mom and dad feel when you give them a big hug or say, "I love you?"

SAY That's just how Jesus feels when we give him our love! Since Jesus' birth is something to celebrate, let's give him the best birthday gift of all—ourselves.

Pass out index cards, markers, and colored pencils to everyone.

SAY In the center of your card, write your name in big letters and decorate it. Add words of love to your card, and make special designs on it. Later, we'll give our cards, which represent ourselves, to Jesus.

 Play "Just Like You Promised" in the background as the kids work. When the cards are finished, set them aside for The Offering.

✳ Christmas Story Luminarias

Give each person a small white paper sack. Set out the bucket of sand and craft supplies on the tables.

SAY While I tell our Bible story today, use these supplies to decorate your sack in a way that tells the story of Jesus' birth. Then, we'll add sand and a candle to each one to make a special Christmas candleholder called a luminaria.

A long time ago, an angel named Gabriel appeared to Mary. He said, "Don't be afraid. God is pleased with you. He's going to give you a special gift. You're going to have a baby, and his name will be Jesus. He'll be the Son of God!" The angel also told Mary that her cousin Elizabeth was going to have a baby too. Mary loved God so much that she said, "I am God's servant. I believe you, and I am willing to do whatever God says."

After the angel left, Mary went to visit Elizabeth. When she got to Elizabeth's house and said "Hello," something odd happened! The baby that was growing inside Elizabeth jumped for joy! That's because Elizabeth and her baby knew that Jesus was going to be born!

Later, Mary and Joseph traveled to Bethlehem. It was time for Mary to have her baby, but all the hotels were full in Bethlehem. So they found a stable, where animals were kept, and they stayed there for the night. That's where Jesus was born! There was no crib in the stable, so Mary and Joseph put the baby Jesus to sleep in a manger. A manger is the trough that holds food for the cows.

Then God sent angels to announce the birth of his Son. They appeared to some poor shepherds who were watching their sheep in a field nearby. At first the shepherds were afraid. But the angel said, "Don't be afraid. I have great news! God's Son has been born in Bethlehem! Go look for a baby sleeping in a manger." Then all the angels started singing for joy. The shepherds ran off to find the baby Jesus. They found him in the stable, and they worshipped him. Then they went and told everyone they knew that God's Son had been born!

ASK • What does the Christmas story tell us about God's love?
• Why is Jesus' birth something to celebrate?
• How will you celebrate Jesus' birth?

When kids have finished decorating their sacks, have each one pour a cup of sand into the bag and place a votive candle inside it.

SAY When you light the candles inside the sacks, the light will glow through them, which is why they're called luminarias. You can give your luminaria to your family for Christmas and tell them the story of Jesus' birth.

(continued on page 53)

Worship Leader Tip

Playing Christmas music softly in the background while you tell the Bible story will help create a peaceful atmosphere in the room. You may want to read the Christmas story from Luke 2 instead of the using the text here.

Preschool Activities 4

The Son of God Is Born! Luke 1:26-45; 2:1-20

Worship Theme: Jesus' birth is something to celebrate.

Using Theo

Consider using Theophilus the FaithRetriever puppet today in these ways:

• Have Theo lead the preschoolers from the main worship area to the preschool room.

• Have Theo distribute the felt ornaments during the "Story Ornaments" activity. Have him watch as the children decorate them and praise them for their efforts.

• See the KidsOwn Worship Kit for a puppet skit written for today's worship session.

✳ Story Ornaments

Before class, cut shapes—circles, diamonds, or hearts, for example—from red felt so that you have one per child. The shapes should be approximately six inches or big enough to hold these decorations: glitter glue, Christmas stickers of baby Jesus and angels or stars, bits of yellow yarn, small cotton balls, and glue. Use a sturdy needle to thread string through each ornament. Tie the string in a loop so children can hang the ornaments.

Have children sit at a table, and give each child a red felt ornament.

SAY Our Bible story today is about Jesus' birth. As I tell it, you can decorate your Christmas ornament. When we finish, your ornament will tell the Christmas story! A long time ago, an angel named Gabriel appeared to Mary. He said, "Don't be afraid. God is pleased with you. He's going to give you a special gift. You're going to have a baby, and his name will be Jesus. He'll be the Son of God!"

Pass out angel or star stickers, and help children put them on their ornaments.

SAY The angel told Mary that her cousin Elizabeth was going to have a baby too. Mary was very surprised. She loved God so much that she said, "I am God's servant. I believe these things will happen."

After the angel left, Mary went to visit Elizabeth. When she got to Elizabeth's house and said, "Hello," something funny happened! The baby inside Elizabeth's tummy jumped for joy! That's because Elizabeth and her baby knew that Jesus was going to be born!

Help children put dots of glitter glue on their ornaments to represent the joy Elizabeth and her baby felt.

SAY Later, Mary and Joseph traveled to Bethlehem. It was time for Mary to have her baby, but all the hotels were full in Bethlehem. So they found a stable, which is where animals live.

Glue bits of yellow yarn to the ornaments. The "hay" can be pressed into a few of the dots of glitter glue or regular glue.

SAY They stayed in the stable for the night, and that's where Jesus was born! There was no crib in the stable, so Mary and Joseph put the baby Jesus to sleep in a manger, where cows eat their hay.

Pass out baby Jesus stickers, and help children place them on their ornament.

SAY Then God sent angels to announce the birth of his Son. He sent them to shepherds who were watching their sheep in a field nearby. Let's glue some little fuzzy balls to our ornament to remind us of the sheep and their shepherds who first heard about Jesus.

Help children glue one or two cotton balls to their ornaments, pressing them into dots of the glitter glue, which should still be wet.

SAY At first the shepherds were afraid. But the angel said, "Don't be afraid. I have great news! God's Son
(continued on page 52)

(continued from page 51)

has been born in Bethlehem! Go look for a baby sleeping in a manger." Then all the angels started singing for joy. The shepherds ran off to find the baby Jesus. They found him in the stable, and they worshipped him. Then they went and told everyone they knew that God's Son had been born!

ASK • Why do we celebrate Jesus' birth?
• What are some ways we can celebrate his birth?

SAY Jesus' birth is something to celebrate! The best way to celebrate is to give our love to him. That's the present he likes best of all. Let's all say, "I love you, Jesus" together. Pause. That's great! I know you just made Jesus happy! And look at the pretty ornaments you made! The decorations on your ornament will help you remember the story so you can tell your family. Then you can hang the ornament on your tree.

> ### Preschool Leader Tip
> Instead of felt shapes, you could use small red or green paper plates for the ornaments. Use a hole punch to make holes for ornament hooks or substitute loops of yarn for the hooks.

Birthday Celebration

You'll need tape and decorations, such as crepe-paper streamers, Christmas lights, and shiny garland, for the classroom. You'll also need paper plates, cups, napkins, juice or water, a frosted birthday cake or cupcakes, and Christmas sprinkles or small red and green candies.

SAY Jesus' birth is something to celebrate, just as you celebrate your birthday.

ASK • How do you celebrate your birthday?
• Why do we celebrate birthdays?
• Why is Jesus' birth something to celebrate?

> ### Preschool Leader Tip
> After the room is decorated, you may want to play the "Musical Cheers" game before giving Jesus his gift and eating the cake.

SAY Let's have a birthday party for Jesus. We'll decorate the room to tell him he's special. Then we'll celebrate and even give Jesus a present!

Have children help you decorate the room. Then let each child add sprinkles or candies to a cupcake.

SAY Before we eat our cake, let's give Jesus presents!

ASK • What kind of present should we give Jesus?

SAY Does Jesus need a toy or a new bathrobe? Does he need food or a nice sweater? No, Jesus doesn't need any of those things. But there is something he wants more than anything else—our love!

ASK • How do your mom and dad feel when you give them a big hug and say, "I love you?"

SAY That's just how Jesus feels when we tell him we love him. Let's give Jesus the best birthday gift of all—our love. Let's say all together, "We love you, Jesus!" Pause. That's great! Let's hug ourselves as if we were hugging Jesus and say it again. Pause. That's just what Jesus wants—your love. Jesus' birthday is something to celebrate! Let's eat our cake now and tell ways your family celebrates Jesus' birthday.

Serve the cake and drinks.

Musical Cheers

You'll need a cassette or CD player, a tape or CD with Christmas songs, two large jingle bells for each child, and twist-ties. Before class, string a twist-tie through each bell.

Help children attach the bells to their shoes by looping the twist-tie through their shoelaces and twisting them. If their shoes don't have anything to fasten the bells to, twist the ties around a finger on each hand to make jingle rings.

Help the children form a big circle.

SAY Let's play a game to celebrate Jesus' birth! While the music is playing, walk around in a circle. As you walk, your bells will make happy sounds to celebrate Jesus' birth. When the music stops, it's time to celebrate! Cheer and clap and dance and do whatever happy thing you want to do to show Jesus that we're happy he was born. Are you ready?

Play Christmas music while the children walk in a circle, starting and stopping the music at intervals. Whenever the music stops, encourage children to express joy and celebrate Jesus' birth with actions and words. After doing this several times, have everyone sit down.

ASK • Why is Jesus' birth something to celebrate?
• How will you celebrate Jesus' birth this week?

SAY Jesus was God's gift to us, and he loves to see us happy about him. Let's keep celebrating all week, even at home. Jesus' birth is something to celebrate!

(continued from page 50)

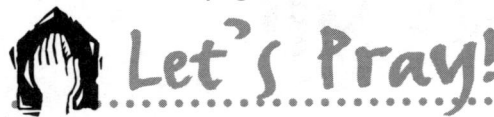

Let's Pray!

The Offering

Gather the children around the tree. Pass out the cards made during the "Presents for Jesus" activity, and place the large gift-wrapped box from Let's Praise God! near you. Give blank cards to the preschoolers.

SAY We learned that the best gift to give Jesus is ourselves. In a minute, we'll pass this gift box around, and you can put your card in it along with your offering, if you brought one today. When you put your card in the gift box, think and pray about giving yourself to Jesus.

ASK • How can our money gifts help others learn about God's gift to us?

SAY Let's celebrate Jesus' birth by giving him our gifts now. As you put your card and offering in the box, tell Jesus silently that you give him your love.

 Sing "Joy to the World!" as the offering box is being passed.

Celebration Cheers

Have kids form small groups of four or five children.

SAY Work with your group to make up a cheer of praise to God that celebrates Jesus' birth. You'll have a few minutes to make up your cheer, then we'll share them with each other. Jesus' birth is something to celebrate, and we're going to celebrate it loud and clear! Give children a few minutes to make up their praise cheers. Then have the groups perform their cheers for each other.

Great cheers, everyone! Those really celebrated Jesus' birth loud and clear! On the count of three, do your cheer one last time. This time, we'll do them all together. Don't think about what the others are doing, just concentrate on saying your cheer to God. Ready? One, two, three!

Celebration Prayers

Have children sit in chairs or on the floor.

SAY Jesus' birth is something to celebrate. Let's celebrate right now with prayer. I'm going to pray, "Thank you, God, for the gift of—" Then you finish the prayer by standing up quickly, saying one word that completes the prayer, and sitting back down again. It's OK to pray more than once, and it's OK if more than one of you pops up at a time. We call that popcorn-style praying, because you pop up randomly, just like popcorn! Let's get our celebration prayers popping!

Say the prayer, and allow enough time for every child to respond.

PRAY God, we thank you for sending Jesus to us! Thank you for giving us something so great and wonderful as your Son to celebrate! We love you and praise you. In Jesus' name, amen.

5

Jesus Grows Up

Luke 2:39-52

Worship Theme: Jesus was amazing.

A Look at the Session

Session Sequence	What Children Will Do	Supplies
Getting Started	Welcome the children to children's church.	**KidsOwn Worship Kit:** *Songs From FaithWeaver, Vol. 6* **Classroom Supplies:** CD player, index cards, pens or pencils
Let's Praise God! 1 (up to 25 minutes)	**Sing:** • "My God Is" (track 4) • "He Is Really God" (track 8) • "We Want to See Jesus Lifted High" (track 19) • "Praise, I Will Praise You, Lord" (track 6) • "Seek Ye First" (track 13)	**KidsOwn Worship Kit:** *Songs From FaithWeaver, Vol. 6;* Lyrics Transparencies **Classroom Supplies:** CD player, overhead projector, wrapping paper, scissors, markers, newsprint

2 Let's Learn the Point! — PRESCHOOL ACTIVITIES (up to 25 minutes)

What Children Will Do	Supplies
✱ **Do You Know?**—Play a game to learn how amazing Jesus is.	
Find Jesus—Learn the story of Jesus in the temple by searching in a picture.	**Classroom Supplies:** Copies of "Find Jesus" (p. 65)
Amazing Teaching—Pretend to be teachers.	**Classroom Supplies:** School props

2 Let's Learn the Point! — ELEMENTARY ACTIVITIES (up to 25 minutes)

What Children Will Do	Supplies
✱ **The Missing Child**—Make "Missing" posters to identify how amazing Jesus was.	**Classroom Supplies:** Paper, markers
✱ **Measuring Up**—Watch a video segment, and discuss being perfect.	**Classroom Supplies:** TV, VCR, *Mary Poppins* video
One and Only—Do a science experiment to see that Jesus was amazing.	**Classroom Supplies:** Clear plastic cups, water, cornstarch, masking tape, markers, pens, paper, pencils, iodine

Session Sequence	What Children Will Do	Supplies
Let's Pray! 3 (up to 10 minutes)	**The Offering**—Offer their gifts to God and tell Jesus he's amazing.	**Classroom Supplies:** Offering bowl
	Amazing Prayer—Use the letters of the word "amazing" to praise God.	
	I Want to Be Like Jesus—Sing praises to God.	**KidsOwn Worship Kit:** *Songs From FaithWeaver, Vol. 6:* "I Want to Be Like Jesus" (track 15) **Classroom Supplies:** CD player

✱ Starred activities can be used successfully with preschool and elementary children together.

Customize your session to fit your needs. You can separate preschoolers and elementary children for Section 2.

Or, if you keep the children all together for the entire worship session, we suggest you choose from the starred activities.

When the twelve-year-old Jesus disappeared, Mary and Joseph finally found him in the Temple. Jesus told them that he had to be about his Father's business. As we become more familiar with what Jesus did during his time on earth, we need to be careful to keep sight of the fact that Jesus truly was and is amazing. He is fully God and fully man, a fact that we can know, yet never completely understand. Use this worship time to remind your children and yourself that we serve a truly amazing God, who completed an amazing plan for our redemption.

Bible Background

Luke 2:39-52

The Bible tells us little of the time between Jesus' dedication at the Temple, when he was an infant, and the event described in this passage, when he was twelve years old. All we know of the period in between is the summary in Luke 2:40. It appears that even in light of his sinless perfection, he developed as a normal child would.

All Jewish males were supposed to worship at the Temple in Jerusalem during Passover, but not all did. Jewish women were not required to go at all. According to Luke 2:41, Mary and Joseph went every year, demonstrating their faithfulness and commitment to God. Their faithfulness indicates the type of home Jesus grew up in.

This visit to Jerusalem was significant because Jesus was twelve years old. He had likely been to the Temple to worship before, but now he was to prepare to take his place in the religious community, which would happen when he turned thirteen.

Modern readers of this account may consider Mary and Joseph irresponsible because they left Jerusalem without knowing that Jesus was with them. However, to understand this event, we must understand the culture. Mary and Joseph were likely traveling in a caravan with lots of other family members. It would have been easy to assume that Jesus was with cousins or other relatives for the day. Some scholars also suggest that adult men and women traveled separately in that culture and both parents could have assumed Jesus was with the other.

It is significant that Jesus was found *sitting* among the teachers. In that culture, a rabbi sat when he taught. The fact that Jesus was sitting might indicate that he was already viewed as a teacher. Luke 2:47 states that the teachers in the Temple were impressed by what he understood and by the answers he gave. This implies that they were asking him questions as well as answering his.

It was natural that Mary and Joseph were extremely worried about Jesus after having looked for him for three or more days. Mary's questioning of him likely stemmed from exasperation and relief. It's interesting to note that Jesus' words to Mary and Joseph are the first of his words to be recorded in the Bible. His question indicates that they had perhaps been reluctant to realize that as he became an adult, he would draw closer to God, even if it meant separating from them. And Luke 1:50 reveals that they still didn't fully understand that this child they had raised was actually the Son of God.

Skits and Puppets

In the KidsOwn Worship Kit, you'll find a collection of skits titled, "KidsOwn Worship Skits." The skits are designed to be used with Theophilus the FaithRetriever puppet during the preschool activities. You can purchase a Theo puppet at your local Christian bookstore.

Song Lyrics and Motions

To make the worship session go more smoothly, tear out the lyrics sheets at the back of this book and keep them in a separate folder. Each week, pull out only the sheets you need for the day's worship session.

Leader SkillBuilder

Thinking about God is a very abstract task, but there are many aspects of God that children wonder about. It is not threatening to their faith development to allow children to express questions about the nature or behavior of God. Encourage children who are having difficulty with this task by asking them "What *is* God like?" "What *do* you know about God?" or similar questions. Then ask them what questions their answers lead them to ask.

Getting Started

Before Worship

Before the worship session, cut wrapping paper into 8x10-inch pieces so you have one for each child and one for yourself. Make sure the paper is not printed on both sides.

Set up a TV and VCR. Rent a copy of *Mary Poppins,* and cue it to the segment that begins thirty minutes and fifteen seconds into the movie. This is the section during which Mary Poppins takes the measuring tape out of her satchel and measures both the children and then herself. This segment lasts about two minutes.

Set up a supply table for the "One and Only" activity. Use masking tape to mark three sections on a long table. You'll need one clear plastic cup for each child. Divide these cups among the three sections. Put plain water in the cups in the first two sections. Make a solution of two teaspoons of cornstarch for every two cups of water for the cups in the third section. In each section, provide masking tape and markers so children can label their cups. Put paper and pencils at one end of the table.

Arrival Time

Play *Songs From FaithWeaver, Vol. 6* as children arrive. Greet children by name, and hand each one an index card and a pencil or pen.

SAY I'm so glad you're here! I would like you to spend a few minutes thinking about God. Please write or draw something about God that you don't understand.

Encourage the older students to assist the younger children with this task.

Let's Praise God!

When all the children have arrived, gather them around you.

SAY When you arrived today, I asked you to think about God and something about God that you don't understand. God is so big that there is a lot we can't understand about him. That only makes what we can understand more special. Today we're going to talk about how amazing Jesus is. Let's sing about some of the amazing things we do know about Jesus.

Sing "My God Is."
Lyrics and motions are in the back of this book.

SAY I would like your help. Let's see how strong you are.

ASK • Who can lift my Bible? Who can lift a chair? Who can lift this table without help? Who can lift this building all by him or herself?

As you ask these questions, allow several children to try each task. Applaud their strength.

ASK • Can you think of anyone who might be able to do all of these things? The children will probably mention sports heroes or fictional action heroes.

SAY Great strength is amazing. But if we're talking about amazing strength, who is the most amazing one of all?

SAY That's right! God is amazing, and Jesus has the same strength because he is really God. The Bible tells us that the Lord is so strong that he holds the universe together. Let's worship him by singing a song that declares, "He is really God."

 **track 8** Sing "He Is Really God."
Lyrics and motions are in the back of this book.

ASK
• Have you ever seen players on a sports team carry one player over their heads at the end of a game?
• Do any of you ever watch the Super Bowl?

SAY At the end of one Super Bowl, the whole team lifted the quarterback high and carried him all the way to the lockers. Tell someone next to you why you think they did that. Allow the children a brief time to share. Then ask for several volunteers to share what their partners told them.

When someone does a very good job, the people who are with him or her might lift the person up as a way to show the crowd that they think this person was amazing. They want the person to be lifted up for all the crowd to see.

ASK
• How do you think Jesus is doing at God's business of holding everything together?

SAY Since we can't touch Jesus to lift him up for everyone to see, let's stand and lift him up with a praise song.

 **track 19** Sing "We Want to See Jesus Lifted High."
Lyrics and motions are in the back of this book.

Let the kids sit down.

SAY Let's learn an amazing trick to help us show another way to lift Jesus up. Sometimes we get so busy that we turn our priorities upside-down, and Jesus doesn't have the proper place in our lives. As you speak, write "Jesus" on the unprinted side of a piece of wrapping paper. Write in big, bold letters with a marker. Show the kids the paper with the word upside-down.

That's no way to serve an amazing God! So we have to pray about that. Fold the paper in half lengthwise by bringing the bottom half up to meet the top half. The word should be on the inside of the paper (see Diagram 1).

And ask for forgiveness for having our priorities out of order. Fold the paper into quarters by bringing the right side over to the left. You should now be holding the fold with your right hand (see Diagram 2).

At this point, we might feel pretty small, admitting that we've been wrong. But that's OK, because we really are sorry. Fold the paper into eighths in the same manner (see Diagram 3).

God forgives us. Lift the top flap. The folded edge should now be in your left hand, folded in quarters (see Diagram 4).

We start to feel better about how things are going. Lift the top flap again, bringing the page back to half (see Diagram 5).

And Jesus is lifted up in our lives. Lift the top part of the paper, revealing the word "Jesus" right side up (see Diagram 6).

Jesus forgives us and sets our lives straight. That's amazing!

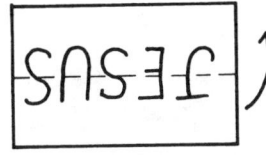
Diagram 1

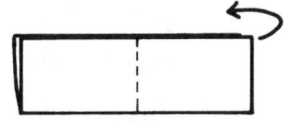
Diagram 2

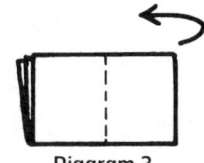
Diagram 3

Diagram 4

Diagram 5

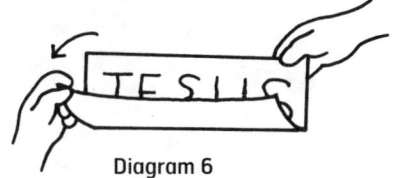
Diagram 6

Give the children wrapping paper, and walk them through the steps of writing Jesus' name and folding the paper. Some children may have difficulty "getting it." If they do, talk about how truly amazing the trick is, and how amazing it is that Jesus can forgive sins. Ask those children who can do the trick to help those who can't after the session, and have the children put the paper aside.

SAY When Jesus sets our hearts right, it's so amazing that we want to praise, love, and serve him. Let's tell God right now that we want to do that with this song.

 Sing "Praise, I Will Praise You, Lord."
Lyrics and motions are in the back of this book.

SAY When people think of serving someone, many people around the world think of serving a king. Tell the person next to you what you think a king or other ruler should be like.

Allow about two minutes to discuss. Then ask for a few children who feel comfortable to share with the group. Write their responses on newsprint.

SAY A king would have to be someone pretty amazing to have all the qualities you listed. And do you know what? Jesus has those qualities. In fact, the Bible calls Jesus the King of kings. He is worthy to rule over us, and he is worthy to rule over all the leaders of the earth. That's amazing! Jesus has an amazing kingdom that he wants all of us to belong to, kids and kings alike.

ASK • Who knows the game Hide and Seek?
• When it is your turn to seek, what do you do?

SAY That's right! You try to find the other people. The Bible tells us we need to seek Jesus' amazing kingdom. When we seek God's kingdom first, God promises that everything else will fall into place. Let's sing that promise from God's Word.

 Sing "Seek Ye First."
Lyrics and motions are in the back of this book.

PRAY God, thank you for your amazing Son, Jesus. Thank you that we can know Jesus. Help us to remember how amazing he is and how wonderful it is to worship such an amazing God. In Jesus' name, amen.

PRESCHOOL ACTIVITIES, pp. 59–60

At this time, have the preschool helper invite the preschoolers to go to their own room for this section of activities. Tear out the Preschool Activities page, and give it to the preschool leader. Have the preschool leader bring the preschoolers back to participate in the prayer time with the older children. If you prefer to keep all the children together, do the starred activities. They will work well with both elementary and preschool children.

(continued on page 61)

Preschool Activities

Jesus Grows Up Luke 2:39-52

Worship Theme: Jesus was amazing.

Using Theo

Consider using Theophilus the FaithRetriever puppet today in these ways:

• Have Theo lead the preschoolers from the main worship area to the preschool room.

• Have Theo ask the children the questions in the "Do You Know?" activity.

• See the KidsOwn Worship Kit for a puppet skit written for today's worship session.

✳ Do You Know?

SAY The Bible tells us that Jesus' body grew and his mind grew. We know he had to learn things just as you do. Let's see how much you are like Jesus. If you think Jesus had to learn to dress himself, stand up. If you had to learn how to dress yourself, sit down. Both you and Jesus had to learn to do that.

If you think Jesus had to learn how to comb his own hair, stand up. If you are learning to comb your own hair, sit down.

If you think Jesus had to learn to read, stand up. If you will have to learn to read, sit down.

Looks like you and Jesus are a lot alike.

If you think Jesus had to eat vegetables to grow strong and tall, stand up. If you need to eat vegetables to grow strong, sit down.

If you think Jesus knew enough to teach the priests and teachers, even though he was a kid, stand up. If you think you could teach the priests and teachers, stay standing.

If you think Jesus made a storm stop, stand up. If you think you could make a storm stop, stay standing.

If you believe that Jesus could create our whole world, stand up. If you believe that you could create our whole world, stay standing.

What you can do is pretty amazing. Jesus learned to do all those things, too, because he was a kid who learned and grew. But Jesus can do things that you will never, ever learn to do because he is God. Jesus is amazing!

ASK • What's something else that Jesus can do that you can't? Respond to each child's answer with "That's amazing!"

SAY Let's find out about one amazing thing Jesus did when he was just a little older than you.

Find Jesus

For this activity, have a copy of the "Find Jesus" handout (p. 65) for each child.

Hand each child a copy of the handout and begin telling today's story from the Bible.

SAY One time, when Jesus was a little older than you, he went on a trip with his parents, Mary

(continued on page 60)

(continued from page 59)

and Joseph. **They may have had a donkey with them, and they might have gone with other people, too. Look on your paper and find Jesus traveling with Mary and Joseph.** If children have trouble finding this, have them look at the bottom of the page near one corner. Continue helping until all children have found the picture.

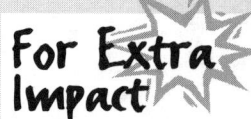

For Extra Impact

To make this activity even more effective for your little ones, have crayons for them to use. Provide four different colors so that they can make each scene of the story a different color.

ASK • **What things do you think they might have taken with them on the donkey for this long trip?**

SAY **When they got to the city called Jerusalem, they went to a place kind of like a church, called a temple, to worship God.**

ASK • **Can you find the temple?** Again help those children who are having trouble by directing them to the middle of the picture.

SAY **After their special time at the temple, everyone who had been with Jesus and his family started back home. Find the people on their way back home.** Direct the children to look on the road going away from the temple to find the group of people.

ASK • **Do you see Jesus with all those people? Mary and Joseph couldn't find Jesus either. They were very worried! They went back to the temple in the city and found Jesus talking to the priests and teachers there.**
• **Can you see Jesus in the temple with all the teachers?**
• **What do you think Jesus is doing there?**

SAY **Jesus was telling the teachers about God. He knew more about God than the teachers at the temple did! That's because Jesus' Father is God. All the teachers thought Jesus was amazing because he knew so much about God. Mary and Joseph thought Jesus was amazing, too.**

Amazing Teaching

SAY **The Bible says that, when Jesus was at the temple, he listened to the teachers and he asked them questions. All of the teachers at the temple were amazed by how much Jesus knew. Jesus knew more than other kids his age knew.**

ASK • **What kinds of things do you suppose Jesus knew?**

SAY **Jesus probably knew so much that he could have taught the temple teachers. Wow! That's amazing. Let's see what it's like to be teachers.**

Work with the children to set up the area to resemble a big kid's classroom. You might want to put chairs in rows facing a blackboard or whiteboard. Then have the children sit at the "desks." Invite the children to take turns pretending to be the teacher. Also, you may want to bring in school props, such as a map or a globe. Give the "teacher" a book, a piece of chalk, or a pointer to point at the map. Have the "teacher" pretend to teach the class. Continue as long as there is interest or until everyone has had a turn.

ASK • **What's it like to be a teacher?**
• **Do you usually see kids being teachers? Why not?**
• **Do you know as much as real teachers know?**
• **What do you think the temple teachers thought when they saw that a little boy named Jesus knew enough to teach them?**

SAY **Jesus was amazing! Even though he was a little boy, Jesus knew as much as the teachers knew. Jesus was different than other children. That's because Jesus is God. Jesus is amazing!**

(continued from page 58)

ELEMENTARY ACTIVITIES

✳ The Missing Child

SAY Today the Bible story we're looking at is about a time when Jesus' parents, Joseph and Mary, lost him.

ASK
- Have you ever been lost?
- What's it like to be lost?
- What do you think it's like for parents when their child is lost?

SAY Listen to what the Bible says about this time. Read Luke 2:41-45 from an easy-to-understand version of the Bible.

ASK
- If this had happened today, what do you think Mary and Joseph might have done to find Jesus?

SAY When a child is lost, his or her parents might circulate posters of the missing child, and they'd probably provide a detailed description to help the authorities locate the missing child.

ASK
- What are some of the things a missing-child poster might include?

SAY Let's make missing-child posters for Jesus. We can't put Jesus' actual photo on a poster, but you can draw a picture of what you think he might have looked like. Then add some things about him that might help people know who he was.

Remember that this was before Jesus' first miracle, so list only things that people might have noticed before he started doing miracles. You can use ideas about what a perfect child might have been like.

Hand out paper and markers. Give the children time to make their posters.

SAY I'd like some of you to share one thing you wrote on your poster. When you've finished reading from your poster, point to the rest of us, and we'll all shout "Jesus is amazing!"

Give the children time to share their posters with one another.

SAY Let's look at the Bible again to see where Joseph and Mary finally found Jesus.

Read Luke 2:46-51. If you'd like, have two of the older children read Mary's comment to Jesus and Jesus' response.

ASK
- What's amazing about this story?
- Why do you think the temple teachers were so amazed by Jesus?
- Do you think Joseph and Mary were surprised by what happened?

SAY The scholars listening to Jesus had studied years and knew the tiniest details of the law. Yet Jesus amazed them with his insight and his understanding. Let's think about what this would be like if it happened today. Let's suppose that it happened at a big university and a twelve-year-old boy was found talking with the professors.

ASK
- Do you think it'd be very likely that university professors would be really impressed with the twelve-year-old? Why or why not?

SAY Jesus was truly amazing—he was amazing even when he was a kid. He amazed his parents, he amazed important teachers, and he amazes us, too. Let's find out more.

✳ Measuring Up

 Watch the video segment from *Mary Poppins*. It shows Mary Poppins measuring the two children and then herself. Stop the video after she says, "Practically perfect in every way."

Then have the children form pairs to discuss these questions. (If the children are organized into small groups, have the small groups discuss these questions.)

ASK • What did Mary Poppins mean when she said the children were practically perfect in every way?
• Do you feel that you're practically perfect in every way? Why or why not?
• The Bible tells us that Jesus lived a perfect life. What does the Bible mean when it says Jesus was perfect?
• What's the difference between saying that we're practically perfect in every way and saying that Jesus was perfect?

After the children have discussed all the questions, regain their attention, and ask volunteers to share their insights with the rest of the large group.

ASK • The Bible tells us that we're supposed to be just like Jesus, who really is perfect in every way. In what ways can we be like Jesus?
• In what ways will we never be like Jesus?

SAY Jesus is amazing because Jesus is God. He truly is perfect in every way. And the Bible tells us to be like Jesus—he's our example of how to live. Along with all the other things that make Jesus amazing is the fact that *he* makes us just like him as we allow him to mold and shape us. Jesus helps us change to be a little bit more like him every day. And that is truly amazing!

One and Only

SAY Jesus must have seemed like any other twelve-year-old boy. But we know that he was different. We know that Jesus was amazing. Let's do a science experiment that'll help us explore that idea. Listen carefully to my instructions. In a moment, I'm going to ask you to form groups of three. Each trio will need to gather one cup of water from each of the three sections on the table. You'll also need a piece of paper and a pencil. You're first job will be to collect evidence. Use masking tape and a marker to label the glasses "one," "two," and "three." Then explore the liquid in the three cups, and determine whether the liquids are alike or different. Use as many of the five senses as you can: you can taste the liquid, smell it, touch it, and look at it. Don't drink the liquid—taste it by dipping your finger in the liquid and tasting your finger. Write down your observations on the piece of paper.

Give the children two minutes or so to study the liquids.

ASK • Are the liquids the same? Did you find anything that's different about any of the liquids?

SAY Now we're going to put a few drops of iodine into each cup. But be careful with the iodine. It's toxic! Do not taste the iodine, and do not taste the liquid in the cups after you've put the iodine into them.

Show the children the iodine.

ASK • **What do you think will happen when we put iodine into the liquid?**

Take the bottle of iodine around the room, and have the children squeeze several drops of iodine into each glass. If you have more than twenty children in your group, you'll want to pour the iodine into several small containers. Put a medicine dropper into each container and have adult or teenage helpers take the small containers of iodine around to trios. Be sure that a responsible person supervises this activity. Allow the children to put the drops of iodine into the cups, but be sure that the adult watches to be sure that the children do not taste or mishandle the iodine.

ASK • **What happened when we put iodine into the liquid in the three cups?**
• **What did you think when you saw what happened?**

SAY At first it looked like the liquid in the three cups was the same stuff—it all looked like plain water. When Jesus came to earth, he must have seemed like a regular person.

ASK • **In what ways was Jesus like everybody else?**

SAY We know that Jesus really was different. Jesus was amazing!

ASK • **In what ways was Jesus different than everybody else—what makes Jesus amazing?**
• **When do you think people started noticing that Jesus was different?**
• **What do you think they thought when they realized that Jesus was different?**

SAY Jesus truly was amazing. Even though he looked like a normal person, he was fundamentally different. That's because he is God. Jesus can do things that other people can't do. Jesus is amazing! Let's learn more about him.

 # Let's Pray!

The Offering

SAY We have talked today about many ways that Jesus is amazing. Right now I want you to think of one way that Jesus is amazing to you. As you come up to the offering bowls today, put your offering in the bowl if you have one, but also pause at the bowl to tell Jesus quietly why you think he is so amazing. After you tell him, silently give Jesus the sign for amazing. Put your hands near your eyes. Make loose fists. Then circle your fists and flick your index fingers and thumbs as you open your eyes wide. Demonstrate the motion. Then have the children walk past the offering bowls.

Amazing Prayer

SAY As we pray today, let's use the word "amazing" to praise God. I'll begin, and then I'll say a letter. You can call out something Jesus is or does that starts with that letter. For example, when I say "A," you might say "awesome," "always with us," or "answers prayers." When we've gone through every letter, I'll close.

PRAY Lord God, you are amazing. We worship you for all the amazing things you are and do. Here are just a few of the things we want to praise you for: A...M...A...Z...I...N...G. Pause long enough for two to four responses to each letter. Then conclude: **You amaze and bless us, Jesus. We want to live in your amazing love, as your followers. In Jesus' name, amen.**

I Want to Be Like Jesus

$AY We have talked about how amazing Jesus is. It's good to want to be like him and amazing that he will help us to do that. Let's sing a prayer to be more like Jesus.

Sing "I Want to Be Like Jesus."
Lyrics and motions are in the back of this book.

After the song, dismiss the children. Ask them to remember to pray and ask Jesus to help them be like him this week.

Find Jesus

OK to copy

Satan Tempts Jesus

Luke 4:1-13

Worship Theme: Jesus never sinned.

A Look at the Session

Session Sequence	What Children Will Do	Supplies
Getting Started	Welcome the children to children's church.	**KidsOwn Worship Kit:** *Songs From FaithWeaver, Vol. 6* **Classroom Supplies:** CD player, poster board, markers
Let's Praise God! 1 *(up to 25 minutes)*	**Sing:** • "We Want to See Jesus Lifted High" (track 19) • "Joy!" (track 5) • "The Good Life" (track 11) • "We Believe in God" (track 10) • "His Love" (track 12) • "That You May Believe" (John 20:31) (track 20)	**KidsOwn Worship Kit:** *Songs From FaithWeaver, Vol. 6;* Lyrics Transparencies **Classroom Supplies:** Bible, CD player, overhead projector, Getting Started lists

2 Let's Learn the Point! — PRESCHOOL ACTIVITIES *(up to 25 minutes)*

What Children Will Do	Supplies
How Long?—Challenge themselves to see how long they can be good at something.	**Classroom Supplies:** Pencils or markers
He Did It For Me!—Fill a poster with "thanks" in response to the Bible story.	**Classroom Supplies:** Poster board, scissors, star or heart stickers
✳ **Temptation Tower**—See that temptation "tips us over" but Jesus never fails.	**Classroom Supplies:** Blocks

2 Let's Learn the Point! — ELEMENTARY ACTIVITIES *(up to 25 minutes)*

What Children Will Do	Supplies
✳ **Resisting Temptation**—Watch a video and discuss the pulls of temptation.	**KidsOwn Worship Kit:** *KidsOwn Worship Video:* "Sucked In" **Classroom Supplies:** TV, VCR, popcorn popper, popcorn, salt, bowl, catalog, Getting Started lists
Sticky Temptation—Run a relay race to see how hard it is to avoid temptation.	**KidsOwn Worship Kit:** Sticky Hands
✳ **Muddy Water, Muddy Lives**—Learn that Jesus remained sinless so he could get rid of their sin.	**Classroom Supplies:** Two clear glasses, water, potting soil, spoon, pitcher

✳ Starred activities can be used successfully with preschool and elementary children together.

Customize your session to fit your needs. You can separate preschoolers and elementary children for Section 2.

Or, if you keep the children all together for the entire worship session, we suggest you choose from the starred activities.

Session Sequence	What Children Will Do	Supplies
Let's Pray! 3 *(up to 10 minutes)*	**The Offering**—Sing a song as they give their offerings.	**KidsOwn Worship Kit:** *Songs From FaithWeaver, Vol. 6:* "I Want to Be Like Jesus" (track 15) **Classroom Supplies:** Offering bowls, CD player
	Picture That Prayer—Draw prayers of praise to Jesus for a sinless life.	**Classroom Supplies:** White sheet, markers, masking tape
	Prayer of Praise—Repeat a prayer of praise to Jesus.	

After forty days in the desert with no food, Jesus was physically weak and vulnerable. Satan chose that moment of weakness for his attack, and he confronted Jesus with three powerful temptations. Yet Jesus refused to give in to temptation. Because of his great love for his Father and us, he made the right choice. Scripture tells us that, because Jesus experienced temptation, he's able to help us face temptation. But Jesus' success over temptation doesn't just provide us with an example of how to live. Because Jesus resisted temptation and lived a perfect life, he was able to pay the price for our sins so that we can live with him forever in heaven. That's reason to worship!

Bible Background

Luke 4:1-13

Jesus was twelve when he left the Temple with Mary and Joseph. When he was baptized, tempted, and began his ministry, he was about thirty (Luke 3:23). That leaves about eighteen years of his life unaccounted for. We can only assume that he spent much of those eighteen years as a carpenter, helping Joseph in the family business (Mark 6:3) and learning about his Father in heaven.

Jesus' temptation by Satan followed closely on the heels of his baptism and God's confirmation of Jesus' relationship with him (Luke 3:21-22). Why did God allow Jesus to be tempted in this way? At least one answer is found in Hebrews 4:14-16. If Jesus had not been tempted as we are, he would not be able to sympathize with our vulnerability to temptation. Because he was tempted, he can identify with us.

Some ask if it was possible for Jesus to give in to Satan's temptations. There's not an easy answer to this question. Some say his divine nature ruled out the possibility of his sinning. Others say that his humanity made him vulnerable to sin and that if the temptation to sin wasn't real, then he wouldn't have been able to atone for our sins in his death. For further study, read Hebrews 2:14-18.

When Satan offered Jesus all the kingdoms of the world, the strength of the temptation was in the shortcut it offered. Satan offered Jesus rule over the world under Satan, who was under God, without having to go through the humiliation and suffering that Jesus knew was coming. The only condition was that Jesus had to worship Satan. But all this was a deception. Jesus wouldn't have become king; he would have become a servant of Satan. And Jesus saw through Satan's plan.

Jesus answered each of Satan's temptations with Scripture. What does that tell us about how we can be prepared to face temptation?

Although Luke 4:1-13 is referred to as "the temptation of Jesus," it's important to remember the words of Luke 4:13. These events didn't mark the end of Satan's attempts to draw Jesus away from God. Throughout Jesus' ministry, Satan tried to capitalize on Jesus' humanity. However, Jesus always withstood the test, and he died for us after living a sinless life.

Skits and Puppets

In the KidsOwn Worship Kit, you'll find a collection of skits titled, "KidsOwn Worship Skits." The skits are designed to be used with Theophilus the FaithRetriever puppet during the preschool activities. You can purchase a Theo puppet at your local Christian bookstore.

Song Lyrics and Motions

To make the worship session go more smoothly, tear out the lyrics sheets at the back of this book and keep them in a separate folder. Each week, pull out only the sheets you need for the day's worship session.

Leader SkillBuilder

During today's various discussions about temptation, look for opportunities to encourage children to think before they act. Read Proverbs 2:12 to them: "Wisdom will save you from the ways of wicked men." Suggest that children ask themselves five questions when they struggle with whether something they want to do is wrong or not: 1) Is it good? 2) Is it right? 3) Does it help someone? 4) Would mom or dad approve? 5) Would Jesus approve? Suggest that they base their actions on the answers to those questions—if the answer to any question is no, they should run the other way. That's wisdom!

Getting Started

Before Worship

Before the worship session, ask one or two adults to help children write things they're tempted by during Getting Started. Each adult helper will need one sheet of poster board and a marker.

 Set up a TV and VCR, and cue the *KidsOwn Worship Video* to the "Sucked In" segment. You'll want to watch the segment at least once before the children arrive so you're familiar with it.

You may want to practice the object lesson for the "Muddy Water, Muddy Lives" activity so you can do it smoothly.

Arrival Time

Play *Songs From FaithWeaver, Vol. 6* as children arrive. Greet children by name, and ask each one to go to an adult helper in the room to add to the list of temptations people face.

Let's Praise God!

SAY **Welcome to children's church, everybody! I need two people to tell us about the best human being they know other than Jesus.** Have two children stand and share with the group.

Those are awesome people! Did you know that no matter how good we are, even if we're as good as Mother Teresa, Abraham Lincoln, or Martin Luther King, Jr., we'll never be perfect? Those people did many good things, but they weren't sinless. The Bible says in Romans 3:23, "for all have sinned and fall short of the glory of God." There is only one person who never ever sinned, and that's Jesus! He is God! Let's stand and worship him by singing "We Want to See Jesus Lifted High."

 Sing "We Want to See Jesus Lifted High."
Lyrics and motions are in the back of this book.

ASK • **Have you ever told a lie? If you have, sit down.** Wait for a moment before continuing.
• **Have you ever disobeyed your parents? If so, sit down.** Wait while children respond.
• **Have you ever been mean to someone? If so, sit down.** Wait while children respond.
• **Have you ever been wrong about something? If so, sit down.** Wait while children respond.

SAY **No one is left standing. Hmm. I guess that means no one here is perfect. I have good news for you—God knows you're not perfect! That's why he sent Jesus. Jesus never sinned, but he died so that we could get to heaven. That's reason to worship with joy!**

 **track 5**   Sing "Joy!"
Lyrics and motions are in the back of this book.

SAY Our next song says, "Look around and see your family, 'cause Jesus made us all one bunch when he came to set us free." Because Jesus never sinned, we get to be part of God's big family! Hug someone near you—or shake someone's hand—and tell your neighbor you're glad he or she is family. Pause while children respond. **Let's worship God and thank him for the good life he gives us because of Jesus.**

 **track 11**   Sing "The Good Life."
Lyrics and motions are in the back of this book.

SAY Jesus never sinned. Because he did everything he was supposed to do on earth, we get to live in heaven forever with him. You might think that it was easy for him to be perfect because he's God. It wasn't. I need a good reader to stand and read Hebrews 2:18 aloud for us. Choose a good reader to read the verse aloud to everyone.

ASK • **What does it mean to be tempted?**
• **How do you feel when you're being tempted?**

SAY The verse tells us that those feelings of fighting temptation are a type of suffering. Jesus felt them too, so he knows just how you feel. That's why he's the perfect one to help you when you're tempted.

Point out the lists of temptations from Getting Started. Quickly read the temptations.

ASK • **Why didn't Jesus ever do anything wrong?**
• **How can Jesus help us when we're tempted?**

SAY When he was on earth, Jesus loved God so much and wanted to please him and obey him. But he had to make choices, just as we do, for good or bad. He knows how hard it is. Jesus never sinned. As we sing our next song, let's lift our hands in the air to symbolize that we're asking for God's help in dealing with temptations. Thank him for never sinning, then believe that he will help you.

 **track 10**   Sing "We Believe in God."
Lyrics and motions are in the back of this book.

SAY Jesus loves us so much. His love is higher than the mountains and deeper than the seas, and it reaches out to you and me. Let's praise and thank him that we don't have to be perfect—he's perfect for us.

 **track 12**   Sing "His Love."
Lyrics and motions are in the back of this book.

SAY Jesus is both God and man. He suffered to do what's right, just as we do. But Jesus never sinned. He never chose the wrong thing. God made sure that verses like Hebrews 2:18 were written down so that we would believe and have life in him. Let's celebrate God's goodness with our last song.

 **track 20**   Sing "That You May Believe" (John 20:31).
Lyrics and motions are in the back of this book.

PRAY Dear Jesus, thank you for never sinning, even though you were tempted just as we are. Thank you for understanding how hard it is to stand strong against temptation. Help us when we need to choose between right and wrong. Thank you for being holy and perfect. We understand how special that is because, no matter how hard we try to do the right thing, sometimes we mess up. We love you, Jesus. In Jesus' name, amen.

Let's Learn the Point!

PRESCHOOL ACTIVITIES, pp. 71-72

At this time, have the preschool helper invite the preschoolers to go to their own room for this section of activities. Tear out the Preschool Activities page, and give it to the preschool leader. Have the preschool leader bring the preschoolers back to participate in the prayer time with the older children. If you prefer to keep all the children together, do the starred activities. They will work well with both elementary and preschool children. ● ● ● ● ● ● ● ● ● ● ➤

ELEMENTARY ACTIVITIES

✳ Resisting Temptation

 Show kids the "Sucked In" segment from the *KidsOwn Worship Video*. It compares the pull of temptation to the gravitational force of a black hole. After the video segment, have the children turn to a partner. Have the pairs discuss the following questions:

ASK • Have you ever faced a temptation that was as strong as a black hole?
• What do you do to stand up against temptation?
• How do you feel when you give in to temptation?
• How do you feel when you resist temptation?

SAY Temptation can be pretty hard to resist, as our video showed. That's what makes today's Bible story so amazing. Jesus resisted incredible temptation. If you have a hot-air popper, begin popping popcorn now.

One time Jesus spent forty days in the desert without eating anything. That's called fasting—not eating anything for a certain amount of time so you can pray to God.

ASK • What's the longest you've ever gone without eating anything?

SAY Forty days without food is a long time! Think about it—that's longer than the time between Thanksgiving and Christmas! Jesus was tired and hungry. That's when the devil showed up and started to tempt him. He knew Jesus wouldn't do anything drastic—he wouldn't steal, kill, or destroy anything. So the devil went a trickier route. He tempted Jesus with food. He said, "Jesus, if you're the Son of God, show off your power, and turn these stones into bread."

Smell that popcorn! We haven't been fasting, and it still smells irresistible! Imagine how Jesus felt at the thought of finally having some food after forty days! Set the popcorn aside when it's finished. Make enough popcorn to allow each child to have a handful at the end of the activity.

(continued on page 73)

Preschool Activities 6

Satan Tempts Jesus Luke 4:1-13

Worship Theme: Jesus never sinned.

Using Theo

Consider using Theophilus the FaithRetriever puppet today in these ways:

• Have Theo lead the preschoolers from the main worship area to the preschool room.

• Have Theo help build the tower in the "Temptation Tower" activity.

• See the KidsOwn Worship Kit for a puppet skit written for today's worship session.

How Long?

You'll need a pencil or marker for each child.

SAY Let's all stand on one foot and see who can do it the longest. As soon as your other foot touches the ground, sit down on the floor with me. Give children time to try this activity one or two times. Then pass out a pencil or marker to each child.

Hold out two fingers of the same hand so they're touching. Now try to balance the pencil across the back of your two fingers. See how long you can balance it. As soon as it falls, come sit on the floor with me. Give children a few moments to practice, then have them try together. Collect the pencils, and have everyone sit down.

Now let's see how long you can sit totally still without even one little wiggle. Is everyone ready? Go! Wait until one or two children wiggle.

Sometimes trying to be good is like the game we just played. We can do it for a little while, and then we mess up.

ASK • How long can you be good?
• What happens sooner or later?
• Can you be good all the time?

SAY As hard as we try, we'll never be good all the time. But there's someone who is—Jesus. Jesus never sinned! That's amazing because we know how hard it is to be good all the time. Let's jump and clap to tell Jesus we think he's awesome!

He Did It for Me!

Before class, cut a large cross shape out of poster board; the shape should be at least 24x18 inches. You'll need a sheet of star or heart stickers for each child.

Have children sit on the floor in a circle.

ASK • Is it hard for you to be good? Tell us about it.

SAY When Jesus was little, he found it hard to be good sometimes too. But he always chose to do the right thing. He never sinned. When he grew up, he still had to choose to be good.

Set the cross on the floor in the center of the circle. Pass out a sheet of stickers to each child.

SAY We're going to use our pretty stickers to tell Jesus thank you for being good. Listen to the Bible story now, and I'll tell you when to pick up your stickers. One time, when Jesus was living on earth, he spent forty days in the desert. Forty days is a long time!

ASK • What's it like in a desert?

SAY The desert is a dry, hot place with lots of sand. While Jesus was in the desert, he didn't eat any food. He got really hungry. Show me how you look when you're really hungry. Pause. The devil came to Jesus and tempted him. That means he tried to get Jesus to do something bad.

(continued on page 72)

(continued from page 71)

ASK • What bad thing do you think he would try to get Jesus to do?

SAY The devil knew Jesus was hungry. He said, "Jesus, show off your power by turning some rocks into bread."

ASK • What should Jesus do?

SAY Jesus knew he shouldn't show off God's power by turning the rocks into bread, so he said "no" to the devil. Obeying God was more important than making food for himself. Jesus chose the right thing! Let's take one of our pretty stickers and put it on the cross to thank Jesus for choosing the right thing. Encourage children to say, "Thank you, Jesus, for doing the right thing," or something similar, as they put stickers on the cross.

Jesus did what was right because he loved God and he loves you! Take one of your stickers and put it on your shirt to show that Jesus said "no" to the devil for you. Pause.

Then the devil tempted Jesus in another way. He led Jesus to a high place where they could see all around. Let's stand up and pretend we're on a high mountain looking all around. Pause. The devil said, "If you worship me, I will give you all the world you can see."

ASK • What should Jesus do?

SAY Jesus knew he shouldn't worship the devil or anyone besides God, so he told the devil that God's Word says to worship only God and no one else. Let's give Jesus another sticker and tell him thank you for doing the right thing. Pause. Now give yourself another sticker because Jesus did it for you. Pause.

That old devil tempted Jesus again! He was sure he could trick Jesus and get him to disobey God! So he took Jesus to the top of a high building. He said, "Prove you're the Son of God. Jump off this high building, and see if the angels will rescue you."

ASK • What should Jesus do?

SAY Jesus knew he shouldn't test God this way, so he said "no" to the devil. Jesus knew that testing God would be wrong. Jesus did the right thing again! Let's give him another sticker and tell him thank you. Pause. Give yourself another sticker because Jesus did it for you! Pause.

Look at all the thanks we've given Jesus! Let's hang our cross in the room to remember that Jesus never sinned.

ASK • What did Jesus say to the devil when he tempted Jesus?
• How can we be like Jesus?

SAY Let's be sure and tell ourselves "No!" when we want to do wrong things. Jesus will help you say "no," because he had to do it too. He did it for you!

Give children the option of decorating the cross or themselves with the rest of their stickers or taking them home.

✳ Temptation Tower

Spread a pile of building blocks on the floor.

SAY Jesus was tempted by the devil to do something bad. Sometimes we are tempted to do bad things too.

ASK • What are some things you are tempted to do?

SAY Let's use these temptations to build a tower with our blocks. We'll pretend each block is a temptation. A temptation means you have to decide if you're going to do something you know you shouldn't do. For example, this block might be the temptation to hit my little brother.

Place the block on the floor. Ask kids to name other temptations they face. For each temptation, have children add a block to the tower until it topples over.

SAY There were so many temptations our tower tipped over! Sometimes it's like that for you and me. We keep trying so hard to do what's right. Then something happens, and we do the wrong thing anyway! Jesus is the only one who never sinned.

ASK • How does it make you feel to know that Jesus never sinned?
• How can Jesus help you say "no" to temptations?
• How does it feel to know that Jesus will help you?

SAY Let's build another tower. This time we'll build it to thank Jesus for helping us. As children add blocks, encourage them to thank Jesus for helping them, For example, a child might say, "Thank you, Jesus, for helping me be nice to my brother," or "Thank you, Jesus, for helping me obey my mom." If the tower hasn't toppled over by the time you finish praying, have one or two children pull out a bottom block so that it falls.

(continued from page 70)

SAY The devil was trying to get Jesus to use his powers in a wrong way. Jesus knew it was wrong. He said to the devil, "Man does not live on bread alone." Obeying God was more important to him than making food for himself.

The devil didn't give up. He led Jesus to a high place and showed him all the kingdoms of the world. He said, "If you worship me, I will give you all these kingdoms."

Show kids a catalog with toys, clothes, and electronics in it.

SAY That would be a little like if the devil showed you this catalog and said you could have it all if you would worship him. Jesus knew he shouldn't worship anyone but God. He told the devil that God's Word says to worship only God and no one else.

So the devil tried another tactic. He led Jesus to the very top of the temple. He said, "Prove you're the Son of God. Jump off this building and see if God's angels come to rescue you."

Jesus knew he shouldn't test God this way, so he told the devil that God's Word says, "Don't test God." The devil finally gave up and went away, knowing he couldn't get Jesus to sin.

ASK • How did Jesus resist the devil's temptations?
• Why is it so amazing that Jesus never sinned?

Point out the lists of temptations the kids made when they arrived.

SAY Jesus resisted temptations much like these his whole life. The difference between Jesus and us is that Jesus never sinned.

ASK • Do you think it was easier for Jesus to say "no" to temptation because he was the Son of God? Explain your answer.

SAY This might surprise you, but Jesus probably had a harder time than you and I do! Think about it: He had all the power to do anything he wanted! You and I don't. But Jesus never took the easy way out! He had power and didn't use it for himself. He was hungry and could have turned rocks into bread. He could have gained a lot of power and glory without having to die for it. But it was the wrong way to get it. He chose not to sin because he loved God and he loved us. That's reason to worship him!

Let's eat this popcorn now and thank Jesus that he never sinned.

Sticky Temptation

Help children form five teams. Have each team sit together in a line on one side of the room so that they'll be ready to run an obstacle course. Have helpers or children quickly set up a line of chairs in front of each team. Make sure the chairs are close together—there shouldn't be more than two or three feet between chairs.

Explain to the children that each team will have one Sticky Hand from the KidsOwn Worship Kit. Each child will have a chance to run the relay race by walking in and out of the chairs as if on a slalom course. As they're walking the race, they *must* swing the sticky part of the Sticky Hand in front of them. The goal is to get all the way through the course without the Sticky Hand getting stuck on anything. Make sure the course is set up so it will be just about impossible for them to accomplish this.

Worship Leader Tip

If you have more than fifty children in your group, you may want to consider breaking into two groups for the next two activities. Have Group 1 do the Sticky Temptation activity, while Group 2 does the Muddy Water, Muddy Lives activity.

Have kids run the relay race. Then collect the Sticky Hands, and put them away.

ASK • **Was it easy or hard to run this race without getting the Sticky Hand stuck on something?**
• **How many of you got the Sticky Hand stuck on at least one chair?**
• **How many of you got the Sticky Hand stuck on the floor or another person or yourself?**
• **Did any of you manage to run the race perfectly, without the Sticky Hand getting stuck?**
• **How was this experience similar to temptation?**
• **Do any of you ever struggle to resist temptation? Is there a situation you could tell us about?**

SAY **Sometimes temptation seems to be everywhere. And sometimes navigating through life without getting caught by temptation seems impossible. Your experience in this game was like trying to stay away from temptation. It's pretty much impossible for us to resist temptation perfectly, but Jesus never sinned. And because he knows what it's like to face temptations, he promises to help you and me when we face them.**

✳ Muddy Water, Muddy Lives

Set two glasses of water on a table where everyone can see them.

SAY **These two glasses of water represent Jesus** (point to the glass on your right) **and us** (point to the glass on the left). Ask a volunteer to put a spoonful of dirt in the glass on the left.

Every time we give in to temptation and sin, it's as if we added dirt to our lives. Have the volunteer add more dirt until the water in that glass turns to mud. **Eventually, our lives and hearts become so dirty, they're like this mud.**

Have the volunteer sit down. Hold up the glass on your right.

SAY **Jesus' life stayed clear and pure because he never sinned. He didn't do that so we would feel bad about ourselves. He stayed pure so he could help us. He wanted to take our sin to himself and get rid of it.**

Pour the mud from the glass on the left into Jesus' glass, and rinse out the empty glass.

SAY **Jesus gave up his own life so he could take all our sin on himself. Then, by the power of God, he got rid of our sin for us.**

Empty and rinse out the glass that represents Jesus. Fill it with fresh water.

SAY **Jesus makes us clean when he forgives our sins. To receive this forgiveness, all we need to do is believe him and ask for it.**

Pour some water from the glass on the right into the glass on the left.

SAY **Jesus never sinned. Because of that, he takes away our sin and fills us with a fresh, clean life. Let Jesus help you say "no" to temptation. He'll help you keep your life clean!**

ASK • **How does knowing that Jesus never sinned make you feel?**
• **How do you feel knowing that Jesus takes your sins and gets rid of them?**
• **How can Jesus help you overcome temptation?**

SAY Let's pray. Thank you, Jesus, for being perfect. Thank you for saying "no" to temptation, then taking our sins and getting rid of them. Please help us keep our lives clean by saying "no" to temptation. Thank you for your love and forgiveness when we fail. In Jesus' name, amen.

 Let's Pray!

The Offering

SAY As we give our offerings, think about Jesus' perfect life. Jesus never sinned. Let's sing during the offering and tell Jesus we want to be like him.

Pass the offering bowls.

 Sing "I Want to Be Like Jesus."
Lyrics and motions are in the back of this book.

Picture That Prayer

Lay a white sheet or a piece of light-colored fabric on the floor.

SAY This cloth represents Jesus' life. Jesus never sinned, so his life stayed clean and pure. To praise him for that, let's write and draw on this cloth to show how we feel about Jesus' sinless life. For example, you might write the word "Amazing!" or draw a picture of two hands clapping. Our drawings will be like prayers to God.

Set out a variety of markers, and encourage children to fill the cloth with prayer pictures. Then ask everyone to stand around the cloth.

SAY Now let's use our pictures to call out prayers to God. We'll tell Jesus what we wrote and drew. This is a way of praising God.

Encourage kids to call out words and descriptions in praise to God. Hang the cloth somewhere in the worship area as a reminder that Jesus never sinned.

Prayer of Praise

SAY We've learned today that Jesus never sinned. Let's praise him one more time for living a sinless life. I'll pray, and you repeat each line after me.

PRAY Jesus, thank you for coming to earth to show us God's love. Pause. Thank you that even though you were tempted, you never sinned. Pause. We praise you for being perfect. Pause. We thank you for saying "no" to temptation. Pause. And we thank you for helping us say "no" to temptation. Pause. We love you forever, Jesus! Pause. In Jesus' name, amen.

7

Jesus Performs His First Miracle

John 2:1-11

Worship Theme: Jesus can do miracles.

Session Sequence	What Children Will Do	Supplies
Getting Started	Welcome the children to children's church.	**KidsOwn Worship Kit:** *Songs From FaithWeaver, Vol. 6;* **Classroom Supplies:** CD player
Let's Praise God! **1** *(up to 25 minutes)*	Sing: • "My God Is" (track 4) • "He Is Really God" (track 8) • "That You May Believe" (John 20:31) (track 20) • "Jesus Loves Me Rock" (track 7) • "We Want to See Jesus Lifted High" (track 19) • "We Believe in God" (track 10)	**KidsOwn Worship Kit:** *Songs From FaithWeaver, Vol. 6;* Lyrics Transparencies; Metal Puzzles **Classroom Supplies:** CD player, overhead projector, newspaper

2 Let's Learn the Point! — PRESCHOOL ACTIVITIES *(up to 25 minutes)*

What Children Will Do	Supplies
✱ **Amazing Colors**—Watch water turn different colors.	**Classroom Supplies:** Vegetable oil, food coloring, clear plastic cups, water, butter knives
Water to Wine—Hear that Jesus turned water to wine, and try to do the same.	**Classroom Supplies:** Pitcher of water, clear plastic cups, spoons
Juice Paintings—Paint a grape juice picture to help them remember the Bible story.	**Classroom Supplies:** Grape juice concentrate, white construction paper, bowls

2 Let's Learn the Point! — ELEMENTARY ACTIVITIES *(up to 25 minutes)*

What Children Will Do	Supplies
✱ **Switcheroo**—Watch milk "turn" into soda.	**Classroom Supplies:** Soda, small cups, milk carton
✱ **Jesus' First Miracle**—Dramatize the Bible story.	**Classroom Supplies:** Butcher paper, markers
Read All About It—Create the front page of a newspaper that tells about Jesus' miracles.	**Classroom Supplies:** Bibles, pens, scissors, newsprint, tape, copy of the "masthead" (p. 86)

✱ Starred activities can be used successfully with preschool and elementary children together.

Customize your session to fit your needs. You can separate preschoolers and elementary children for Section 2.

Or, if you keep the children all together for the entire worship session, we suggest you choose from the starred activities.

Session Sequence	What Children Will Do	Supplies
Let's Pray! **3** *(up to 10 minutes)*	**The Offering**—Listen to a song and pray while the offering is collected.	**KidsOwn Worship Kit:** *Songs From FaithWeaver, Vol. 6:* "He Is Really God" (track 8) **Classroom Supplies:** Offering bowls, CD player
	Prayer Cheer—Offer cheers of praise to Jesus.	
	Closing Prayer—Offer a closing prayer.	

Why We Worship

Kids idolize superheroes who tackle feat after feat of derring-do. But kids do realize that these idols aren't real and that no one can really do the kinds of things that Superman, Batman, and Spider-Man do in comic books and on TV. This is your chance to tell kids about a real, living Superhero who really can do amazing feats. Jesus can do miracles. There's nothing that's too hard for him to do. He has power over all of creation. Have fun telling kids about Jesus' ability to do amazing things, and enjoy this time of worship.

Bible Background

John 2:1-11

Early in Jesus' ministry, Jesus and his disciples were invited to a wedding. While they were at the party that followed the wedding, the wine began to run out. Such an error would have been considered a significant social blunder at that time. Even a poor groom was expected to provide plenty of wine for his wedding party. This setting provided the occasion for Jesus' first miracle.

Mary may have been helping to serve at the wedding; thus, her appeal to Jesus was for herself as well as for the host of the party. Though some suggest that she was asking Jesus to go out and get more wine, it is more likely that she expected Jesus to do something miraculous.

When Jesus addressed his mother as "dear woman," he was not rebuking her, as it may seem; rather his words demonstrated respect. The rest of that sentence, though the exact translation is debated, appears to mean, "Your concern and mine are not the same." When he said, "My time has not yet come," Jesus was likely indicating that the proper time had not yet come for his first miracle, though it was coming. The point was that he would not be hurried, not even by his mother. The time for Jesus to be revealed as the Messiah and then to be crucified had not yet arrived.

When the master of the banquet tasted the wine, he was astonished. The quality of the wine simply reinforced the wonder of the miracle. And Jesus' "disciples put their faith in him" (John 2:11b).

Skits and Puppets

In the KidsOwn Worship Kit, you'll find a collection of skits titled, "KidsOwn Worship Skits." The skits are designed to be used with Theophilus the FaithRetriever puppet during the preschool activities. You can purchase a Theo puppet at your local Christian bookstore.

To make the worship session go more smoothly, tear out the lyrics sheets at the back of this book and keep them in a separate folder. Each week, pull out only the sheets you need for the day's worship session.

Getting Started

Before Worship

Before the worship session, recruit a volunteer to help you with the "Switcheroo" activity. Wash out a milk container, fill it with soda, and use a glue stick to seal the container so that it looks unused. Put the container in a refrigerator that will be accessible to your volunteer. For "Jesus' First Miracle," prepare six sheets of butcher paper by drawing water jugs on both sides of each sheet. On each sheet, write "water" on one jug and "wine" on the other.

For "Read All About It," divide a sheet of newsprint (or several sheets) into newspaper-article-shaped pieces. You'll want a piece for every three or four children. If you use more than one sheet, be sure the pieces are interchangeable from one sheet to another.

Arrival Time

Play *Songs From FaithWeaver, Vol. 6* as children arrive. Greet children by name, and welcome them to children's church.

Let's Praise God!

SAY Hello, everyone! Welcome to children's church. Let's start our worship session by singing about who God is.

Sing "My God Is."
Lyrics and motions are in the back of this book.

SAY It's really true that Jesus gives us hope and salvation. Jesus created the world: He made the land and the sea, and he gives us hope and salvation. Today we're going to be celebrating something else about Jesus. Here's a clue about our theme for today.

Hold up a Metal Puzzle from the KidsOwn Worship Kit.

Help children form twelve groups, and give each group a puzzle. If you already have children in small groups, simply give each group a puzzle. If you have more than twelve groups, have some of the groups get together for this activity.

Tell the children to take turns trying to figure out their group's puzzle. Give the groups three or four minutes to try.

ASK • Did anyone figure out the puzzle?
• What does it take to be able to figure out these puzzles?
• Do you think Jesus could do these puzzles?
• Why do you think Jesus could easily do these puzzles—what makes Jesus different from us?

SAY We worship Jesus because he is God. Jesus is better at everything than we are. He's stronger and smarter than we are. Jesus can do anything, even miracles. Let's sing about Jesus.

Sing "He Is Really God."
Lyrics and motions are in the back of this book.

SAY Let's talk about miracles for a bit.

ASK • What exactly is a miracle?
   • Why can Jesus do miracles?
   • Can people do miracles? Why or why not?

SAY When something truly impossible happens we call it a miracle. Jesus can do miracles—Jesus can do the impossible. The Bible tells us about many miracles that Jesus did to help us believe in him. Let's sing about that.

 Sing "That You May Believe" (John 20:31).
Lyrics and motions are in the back of this book.

ASK • Why do you think Jesus does miracles?

SAY One reason might be because he loves us. The miracles Jesus did in the Bible help us to believe in him. They help us know who he really is. Jesus knows that it's really important for us to believe in him. Let's sing about Jesus' love.

 Sing "Jesus Loves Me Rock."
Lyrics and motions are in the back of this book.

SAY Jesus does miracles because he loves us and because he wants to help us. We worship Jesus because he *can* do miracles and because he *does* do miracles. Jesus' miracles help us see that he really is special. Doing miracles is something that only God can do. Since Jesus can do miracles, we know that he is God.

And here's one more reason why Jesus does miracles.

Show the children the front page of your local newspaper.

ASK • What kind of news gets put on the front page of the newspaper?

SAY The most important stories are on the front page of the newspaper. More people see what's on the front page of the newspaper than what's buried on the back page. Jesus' miracles are "front-page" news. Turn to your neighbor, and tell him or her a headline you might expect to see if newspapers had been around to write about Jesus.

Give the children a moment to share with their neighbors.

SAY Jesus does miracles so that more people will hear about him and more people will believe in him. Jesus' miracles make people pay attention to him. We want people to see Jesus lifted high above all other people. Let's sing about that.

 Sing "We Want to See Jesus Lifted High."
Lyrics and motions are in the back of this book.

SAY Jesus really is the only way to heaven. So we know that we all need Jesus. Let's sing "We Believe in God" as a prayer to tell God that we do believe in Jesus and the miracles he does.

 Sing "We Believe in God."
Lyrics and motions are in the back of this book.

Let's Learn the Point!

PRESCHOOL ACTIVITIES, pp. 81-82

At this time, have the preschool helper invite the preschoolers to go to their own room for this section of activities. Tear out the Preschool Activities page, and give it to the preschool leader. Have the preschool leader bring the preschoolers back to participate in the prayer time with the older children. If you prefer to keep all the children together, do the starred activities. They will work well with both elementary and preschool children.

ELEMENTARY ACTIVITIES

✳ Switcheroo

SAY **All of the singing we've done today has made me thirsty. Let's take a break and have something cold to drink.**

Bring out a bottle of soda pop and small cups, and put them on a table at the front of the room. Be sure you only have enough soda to serve about half of the students. Invite the volunteer you talked to before the worship session to come and pour the drinks. Invite a few other children to serve the drinks to the children. While the soda is being poured and served, help the children talk about miracles.

ASK • **Have you ever seen a miracle? Tell us about it.**
• **What exactly is a miracle?**
• **Can people do miracles, or can only God do miracles? Explain.**
• **Why do you think Jesus did miracles?**
• **Why is it important that Jesus could do miracles?**

When the soda is gone, have the volunteer get your attention and ask what to do. Tell the volunteer to look in the church kitchen to see if there's more soda. While the volunteer goes to the kitchen, continue talking with the children about miracles.

When the volunteer returns, he or she will have the milk carton that you prepared before class. Have the volunteer apologize loudly that there was no more soda in the kitchen, but there was milk. Tell the volunteer that it's OK—some of the children will just have to drink milk instead of soda.

Have the volunteer make a big production of opening the milk container and pouring the contents into the cups. Then have the volunteer exclaim loudly enough to interrupt the discussion you're having with the children. The volunteer should say something like, "Oh my! I can't believe it. It must be a miracle. I expected to see milk. But there's soda pop in this milk carton. How can this be?" Have the volunteer continue pouring soda from the milk container into cups until every child has a cup.

SAY **This reminds me of a Bible story. I'll need six kids to help me tell the story.**

✳ Jesus' First Miracle

Choose six children to stand at the front of the room. Give each child a sheet of the butcher paper you prepared before class, and have the children hold the paper so the "water" side shows. Whisper to them that when you pretend to dip a cup into one of the water pitchers, they should quickly turn the papers over to show the wine side.

(continued on page 83)

Preschool Activities

Jesus Performs His First Miracle John 2:1-11

Worship Theme: Jesus can do miracles.

Using Theo

Consider using Theophilus the FaithRetriever puppet today in these ways:

• Have Theo lead the preschoolers from the main worship area to the preschool room.

• Have Theo help count the glasses in the "Water to Wine" activity.

• See the KidsOwn Worship Kit for a puppet skit written for today's worship session.

✳ Amazing Colors

You'll need vegetable oil, liquid food coloring, and water, as well as a clear plastic cup and a butter knife for each child.

Before the session, pour roughly equal amounts of water and vegetable oil in the plastic cups, filling them about two thirds full. Set the cups aside to let the oil and water settle into two distinct layers.

Give each child a cup with layers of oil and water, and allow the children to squirt drops of food coloring into the cups. The food coloring, which is water-based, will collect in little beads on the oil. Show the children how to use the butter knives to gently push the beads of coloring through the oil to the water layer. Once the coloring touches the water, it will immediately mix with the water and color it. As the water is colored, make comments such as, "Isn't that amazing?" and "Oh, the colored water is so pretty."

Place the glasses in a windowsill or somewhere else where the children can admire the colors.

ASK • What happened when you squirted the food coloring into the glass?
• What happened when you pushed the little beads of coloring down to the bottom?

SAY Wasn't it amazing how the water suddenly turned a different color? Today our Bible story is about an amazing miracle that Jesus did. Jesus turned water into something completely different. Let's find out what happened.

Water to Wine

You'll need a pitcher of water, clear plastic cups, and spoons.

SAY One day Jesus went to a wedding.

ASK • Have you ever been to a wedding?
• What happens at a wedding?

You may want to choose children to pretend to be a bride, a groom, and a minister, and have the children act out a wedding. Other children can be the guests or the bridesmaids and groomsmen. The children may want to act this out several times, with different children as the bride and groom each time.

SAY Sometimes, after the bride and groom get married, all the wedding guests celebrate with a great big party. Jesus went to a party after the wedding he attended. But a bad thing happened at the party. They ran out of wine to drink.

ASK • What would you think if you went to a birthday party and they ran out of cake before you got your piece?

(continued on page 82)

(continued from page 81)

SAY That's just how the people at the wedding would've felt. So Jesus decided to help. He told the servants to bring him six water jugs. Let's pretend these cups are the water jugs.

Have the children count out six plastic cups.

Jesus told the servants to fill the jugs with water.

Fill the glasses with water. If you have a small plastic pitcher, you may want to have the children fill the glasses with water.

SAY Then Jesus told the servants to dip some out and give it to the host of the party. When the host took a sip, he tasted wine instead of water.

Have the children use the spoons to dip out some of the water and taste it.

ASK • Did our water turn to wine? Why not?

SAY Maybe if we try really hard, we'll be able to turn the water into wine. Let's try it.

Have the children concentrate on turning the water into wine.

ASK • Did anything happen? Did the water turn into wine? Why not?
• Why did the water turn into wine for Jesus?

SAY Jesus is God. Jesus can do miracles. We can't do miracles because we aren't God. Let's praise God for being able to do miracles. Let's all say "Praise Jesus!"

Juice Paintings

You'll need white construction paper and grape juice concentrate. Put the concentrate in shallow plastic bowls.

Encourage the children to paint a picture on the white construction paper with the grape juice concentrate. The children can dip their thumbs in the concentrate and paint with their thumbs. If the children don't want to have purple thumbs, you can provide cotton swabs or paintbrushes for them to use.

It's best to use construction paper instead of typing paper for this activity. Construction paper will absorb the juice better and make a prettier picture.

While the children are painting talk about the story. Encourage them to smell their pictures. Talk about how the wine would've smelled like grape juice. Encourage them to taste the grape juice. Ask them if the grape juice tastes the same or different than water. Talk about how the wine would have tasted a bit like grape juice.

SAY Jesus turned water into wine. Jesus can do miracles. You might not be able to do miracles, but you painted beautiful pictures. Take your pictures home, and tell your families about how Jesus turned water into wine.

(continued from page 80)

SAY One day Jesus was at a wedding. At this wedding, the hosts ran out of wine, just as we ran out of soda pop. It was a terrible, embarrassing thing to run out of wine. It would have been like inviting people to your house for dinner, then running out of food before everyone had their first helping.

Jesus' mother asked him to do something about the problem. So Jesus said, "See those water jugs?" Point to the six children holding the butcher paper. "Fill them with water." And so the servants filled the jugs with water. Let's make water noises to show that the water jugs have been filled with water. Lead the children in saying, "Glug, glug, glug, glug." You may want to have the six children crouch near the floor and stand up slowly as the group says, "Glug, glug, glug, glug" to indicate that the jugs are being filled with water.

Then Jesus told the servants to draw some water out of a jug and give it to the banquet master. The servants did just as Jesus said. Pretend to dip into one of the jugs with an empty cup, and have the children turn their papers over quickly. Take the empty paper cup to the volunteer who poured the soda earlier in this activity. And the banquet master said, "This stuff is great! Most people serve the best wine first and then they bring out the cheap stuff. But you've saved the best wine until last."

Jesus had turned the water into wine. This was the first miracle that Jesus did. Let's applaud our water jugs to thank them for helping tell the story.

Lead the children in applauding the six volunteers, then have the volunteers sit down.

ASK • What do you think the servants thought when they saw the water had turned into wine?
• What do you think the servants thought about Jesus when they saw this miracle?
• Why do you think Jesus did this miracle?
• Do you think it was easy or hard for Jesus to do this miracle? Explain.

SAY This was the very first miracle that Jesus did. And it amazed Jesus' followers. Even today, when we hear about this story, we're amazed. God is the only one who can really do a miracle. This miracle shows that Jesus was God. Let's learn more.

Read All About It

Have children form small groups of three or four. Assign each group one of the following Scriptures and the question that goes with it.

• John 10:25—What do Jesus' miracles tell us about him?

• Romans 15:18-19—Why do miracles help us believe in Jesus?

• Hebrews 2:3b-4—Why do you think God wanted us to know about salvation so much that he proved it through miracles?

Give the groups several minutes to discuss the video segment and the Scripture passage they've been assigned. Then ask for individuals to share their small group's insights with the entire group.

SAY Miracles help us believe in Jesus. And they help spread the news about the amazing God that we serve. We worship Jesus because he is God—and part of being God is the ability to do miracles. Let's think about how we can spread the news about Jesus to others.

Hand out the pieces of newsprint you prepared before the worship session so that each small group has one piece. Also give each group a colored pen or pencil. Make sure Bibles are available, too.

Explain to the children that they are to look through the Gospels, choose one of Jesus' miracles, and write a short news article (or draw a picture and write a short cutline) about it on the sheet of paper they've been given. Tell them to think of a headline for their story first and write it at the top of the block. Under the headline, have them include the facts about the miracle and its significance—why they think Jesus did the miracle, how the people reacted to the miracle, and how we can react to the miracle today.

Give the children ten minutes to work on their news article or picture. Then get the groups' attention, and have each group read its article. If you have more than five or six groups, you may just want to have someone in each group tell what miracle the group wrote about and why.

Have each group bring its article to the front of the room. Tape the articles to a sheet of fresh newsprint to form the front page of a newspaper—it's OK if all the text doesn't go the same direction. Be sure to photocopy the masthead from page 86 and tape it at the top of the front page. (See the example in the margin.)

Show children the finished newspaper. Read aloud the title of the newspaper from the masthead, and read the verse printed underneath the title.

ASK • What have you learned about Jesus and the miracles he's done?
• Why are Jesus' miracles such a big deal?

SAY Jesus' miracles are a very big deal. They show us that Jesus is God, and they show us how much he loves us and cares about us. Think about the miracles Jesus did. Every single one of them was done to help people. Jesus' miracles show us and the entire world how great he really is.

Let's Pray!

The Offering

While you take the offering, play the song "He Is Really God." Tell the children to think about Jesus' miracles while they listen to the song.

SAY While you're waiting for the offering bowl to come to you, think about the words of this song and silently pray to Jesus. Thank him for the miracles he's done, and praise him for being able to do miracles.

Prayer Cheer

SAY The Bible tells us that Jesus' followers began to praise God joyfully for all the miracles they'd seen. Now, it's our turn to praise Jesus joyfully for all the miracles he's done.

Draw an imaginary line down the middle of the room and indicate that all the children on one side of the line are Group 1. All the children on the other side are Group 2. Explain that individuals will come to the front of the room and call out a miracle that Jesus did. Then Group 1 will call out "Jesus can do miracles." Group 2 will respond by calling out, "Nothing is impossible with God."

Invite volunteers to come to the front to call out a miracle. Have the two groups respond to each miracle by calling out their lines.

After children have responded to several miracles, have them praise Jesus with applause and cheers—"Thank you, Jesus" and "We praise you, God," for example.

Closing Prayer

Ask one of the children to close the worship session in prayer, or pray yourself.

PRAY Dear Jesus, today we praise you because you can do miracles. You are a great and mighty God, and nothing is too difficult for you. We thank you for doing miracles to teach us about who you are. And we thank you for doing miracles to help us believe in you and understand the salvation that you offer us. Thank you, Lord Jesus. In your name, amen.

Vol. 1
January 14, 2001

"A Glad Tidings Newspaper"

Miracle Watch News

"But these are written that you may believe that Jesus is the Christ, the Son of God, and that by believing you may have life in his name" (John 20:31).

Jesus Teaches in a Synagogue

Luke 4:14-21

Worship Theme: Jesus helps hurting people.

A Look at the Session

Session Sequence	What Children Will Do	Supplies
Getting Started	Find a warm welcome at children's church.	**KidsOwn Worship Kit:** *Songs From FaithWeaver, Vol. 6* **Classroom Supplies:** CD player
Let's Praise God! *(up to 25 minutes)* 1	Sing: • "Joy!" (track 5) • "My God Is" (track 4) • "His Love" (track 12) • "Jesus Loves Me Rock" (track 7) • "He Is Really God" (track 8) • "Praise, I Will Praise You, Lord" (track 6)	**KidsOwn Worship Kit:** *Songs From FaithWeaver, Vol. 6;* Lyrics Transparencies **Classroom Supplies:** CD player, overhead projector, transparency of Isaiah 61:1-3a (p. 90)

2 Let's Learn the Point! — PRESCHOOL ACTIVITIES *(up to 25 minutes)*

What Children Will Do	Supplies
Helping Others' Hurts—Care for stuffed animals, and pretend to be Jesus as they care for one another.	**Classroom Supplies:** Stuffed animals, blankets, first-aid kit
Jesus Came to Help—Explore the Bible story by acting it out.	**Classroom Supplies:** Bible
Frowns to Smiles—Make a craft that changes from a frowning face to a smiley face.	**Classroom Supplies:** Paper plates, markers, paper fasteners, yarn, scissors

2 Let's Learn the Point! — ELEMENTARY ACTIVITIES *(up to 25 minutes)*

What Children Will Do	Supplies
✳ **A Celebrity Visit**—Talk about having a celebrity come to visit and explore the Bible story.	**Classroom Supplies:** Overhead projector, Isaiah 61:1-3a transparency from Let's Praise God!
✳ **Tears of Sadness**—Create a wailing wall of hurting people and see that Jesus helps them.	**Classroom Supplies:** Blue tissue paper, scissors, mural paper, tape, pencils, spray bottle, water
✳ **Sharing Comfort**—Hear about Jesus' comfort, and pass comfort on to others.	**Classroom Supplies:** Bible

Session Sequence	What Children Will Do	Supplies
Let's Pray! *(up to 10 minutes)* 3	**The Offering**—Ask Jesus to use the offering to help hurting people.	**KidsOwn Worship Kit:** *Songs From FaithWeaver, Vol. 6:* "My God Is" (track 4) **Classroom Supplies:** Offering bowls, CD player
	Teardrop Prayers—Pray for people who are hurting.	**Classroom Supplies:** Wailing wall from "Tears of Sadness" activity
	Sorrow Into Dancing—Talk about what God turns sorrow into and sing a praise song.	**KidsOwn Worship Kit:** *Songs From FaithWeaver, Vol. 6:* "Joy!" (track 5) **Classroom Supplies:** CD player

✳ Starred activities can be used successfully with preschool and elementary children together.

Customize your session to fit your needs. You can separate preschoolers and elementary children for Section 2.

Or, if you keep the children all together for the entire worship session, we suggest you choose from the starred activities.

Why We Worship

Isaiah prophesied that the coming Messiah would "preach good news to the poor...bind up the brokenhearted, proclaim freedom for the captives...[and] comfort all those who mourn." Jesus did all of these things and more. Jesus is the promised Messiah. He is compassionate, kind, and loving. Jesus helps people. That is certainly good reason to worship him, the Son of God, our Redeemer and Lord, Jesus Christ.

Skits and Puppets

In the KidsOwn Worship Kit, you'll find a collection of skits titled, "KidsOwn Worship Skits." The skits are designed to be used with Theophilus the FaithRetriever puppet during the preschool activities. You can purchase a Theo puppet at your local Christian bookstore.

Bible Background

Luke 4:14-21

News about Jesus had begun to spread. The verb tense in Luke 4:15 indicates that Jesus taught in the synagogues regularly. So this occurrence in Nazareth was not unusual because it took place; it was unusual because of what Jesus said when he taught there.

One might wonder why Jesus was allowed to teach in the synagogue. Any Jewish male was allowed to speak if he notified the leader of the synagogue in advance. The fact that the scroll of Isaiah was given to Jesus to read may be considered a coincidence, but it was more likely arranged by God.

It was customary for the Scripture reader to stand when reading from the scrolls, out of respect for God's Word. The reader then sat down and, if he so desired, commented on what he'd read. Jesus' choice of the passage from Isaiah 61:1-2 about the Messiah wasn't unusual. It was Jesus' commentary that shocked his listeners. He clearly announced that he was the promised Messiah (Luke 4:21), an idea that was not well received by those with whom he had grown up. To them he was just the son of a carpenter, not the glorious Messiah-king they were hoping for. No matter what miracles he had done or how insightfully he taught, they just could not believe that this hometown boy was the Messiah.

The qualities and actions in Isaiah 61:1-2 that Jesus ascribed to himself are the very same qualities that attract most people to Jesus. These verses tell us who Jesus came to help: the poor, the captive, the disabled, and the oppressed. He came to help all of us who are imprisoned by sin and to set us free through faith in him.

 # Getting Started

Song Lyrics and Motions

To make the worship session go more smoothly, tear out the lyrics sheets at the back of this book and keep them in a separate folder. Each week, pull out only the sheets you need for the day's worship session.

Before Worship

Before the worship session, copy the box on page 90 (Isaiah 61:1-3a) onto a transparency.

Arrival Time

Play *Songs From FaithWeaver, Vol. 6* as children arrive. Greet children by name, and say to each one, "Hello! Welcome to children's church."

 # Let's Praise God!

SAY Hello, everyone! Welcome to children's church. I'm so glad you're here today. To begin our worship time together, we're going to have a Sad Story Jamboree. Your job is to make up the saddest, funniest story you can, and tell us about it. Here's one to get you thinking.

One night I stayed up late decorating a wedding cake. I stayed up so late, I overslept the next day and had to rush to get the cake to the church for the wedding. I didn't even have time to put on my clothes. I took the cake to the car, and I jumped in the car—still in my bathrobe—and took off. When I got to the church, the cake wasn't in the car. I drove home thinking I'd forgotten it. When I got home, I saw my beautiful cake smashed in the driveway. I drove back to the church. There were the bride, the groom, and all the guests. I stood there in my bathrobe crying, and I explained that there would be no wedding cake because it had fallen off the roof of my car because I'd forgotten to put it inside the car.

Explain to the children that they should respond by saying, "poor, poor pitiful you." Invite several of the children to make up stories and tell them to the group. After a child shares a story, have the rest of the group respond by saying "poor, poor pitiful you."

SAY It was a lot of fun telling these sad stories, but we all know that bad things really happen to people all the time. People get hurt, or they get sick, or their families fight, or they struggle in school. Life isn't always easy. The good news is that Jesus came to help hurting people. Jesus helps hurting people and gives them joy. Let's sing about joy.

 Sing "Joy!"
Lyrics and motions are in the back of this book.

SAY Look what the Bible says about Jesus. Let's read the words together.

Show the transparency of Isaiah 61:1-3a on the overhead projector. Read the words aloud with the children.

"The Lord has appointed me to tell the good news to the poor.

He has sent me to comfort those whose hearts are broken, to tell the captives they are free, and to tell the prisoners they are released.

He has sent me to announce the time when the Lord will show his kindness and the time when our God will punish evil people.

He has sent me to comfort all those who are sad and to help the sorrowing people of Jerusalem.

I will give them a crown to replace their ashes, and the oil of gladness to replace their sorrow, and the clothes of praise to replace their spirit of sadness."

(Isaiah 61:1-3a, NCV)

SAY Jesus is all this and more. Let's sing about all that Jesus is.

 Sing "My God Is."
Lyrics and motions are in the back of this book.

SAY Think about when you were hurting, sad, or lonely. Remember how it felt to be so sad.

ASK • What comforts you when you feel sad or lonely?
• Why do you suppose it's important to Jesus to help hurting people?

SAY I think one reason Jesus helps hurting people is because he loves us. Let's sing about Jesus' love.

 Sing "His Love."
Lyrics and motions are in the back of this book.

SAY Jesus loves us more than anyone else does. He wants to comfort us when we're sad and hurting. When bad things happen to us, we can know that Jesus is right there waiting to help us. Listen to what the Bible says happens to our sorrow when we ask Jesus for help. "You changed my sorrow into dancing" (Psalm 30:11a, NCV). Let's sing about Jesus' love again. But this time, let's dance to show that Jesus really does turn our sorrow into dancing. While you're singing and dancing, concentrate on how much Jesus loves you.

 Sing "Jesus Loves Me Rock."
Lyrics and motions are in the back of this book.

ASK • What does Jesus do to help people when they are hurting?
• How can Jesus help so many people?

SAY When Jesus grew up and began his ministry, people wondered if he could be the Messiah that God promised all through the Old Testament. Jesus told the people that he was the one God promised to send. He was the one who would help sad people and heal sick people. He explained that he came to save people. He explained that he is really God. That's why Jesus can help people. Let's praise Jesus because he is really God.

 Sing "He Is Really God."
Lyrics and motions are in the back of this book.

SAY Think about a time you were hurting and Jesus comforted you. Let's all be very quiet for a moment. In your heart, thank Jesus for comforting you and giving you peace and joy instead of pain and sorrow. If you're hurting about something right now, tell Jesus about it. Then remember how much Jesus loves you and wants to help you. Ask Jesus to help you and give you comfort.

Pause for a moment to allow the children to pray.

SAY Now let's praise Jesus with all our hearts, remembering that we find the source of all our joy in Jesus.

 **track 6**   Sing "Praise, I Will Praise You, Lord."
Lyrics and motions are in the back of this book.

PRAY Lord Jesus, we thank you for coming to our world. And we thank you for coming to help us. Sometimes we feel brokenhearted. The Bible says that you came to comfort brokenhearted people. Sometimes we feel sad. The Bible says that you came to comfort sad people. Thank you for turning our sadness into joy and dancing. In your name, amen.

Let's Learn the Point!

PRESCHOOL ACTIVITIES, pp. 93–94

At this time, have the preschool helper invite the preschoolers to go to their own room for this section of activities. Tear out the Preschool Activities page, and give it to the preschool leader. Have the preschool leader bring the preschoolers back to participate in the prayer time with the older children. If you prefer to keep all the children together, do the starred activities. They will work well with both elementary and preschool children.

ELEMENTARY ACTIVITIES

✳ A Celebrity Visit

ASK • Who's your favorite movie star? singer? sports figure?

SAY Let's pretend that we can invite one famous person to come to our town and meet with us.

ASK • Who should we invite?

Have the children vote on which celebrity they'd like to invite.

ASK • How do you think we should prepare for [celebrity's name]'s visit?
• If we were to invite [celebrity's name] to our town, what do you think [he or she] would do when [he or she] came?
• If [celebrity's name] were to give a speech, what do you think it would be about?

SAY It'd be a lot of fun to meet and talk to a celebrity. The Bible tells us about a celebrity showing up in his own hometown. Here's what happened.

Jesus traveled around the countryside teaching people and healing people. He was famous. One day Jesus went to the synagogue in his hometown, a tiny

For Extra Impact
If your town has produced a famous person—an astronaut, musician, or politician, for example—gather information about that person, and talk about times when the celebrity has returned to your town. Talk about what it's like to live in the town where a celebrity grew up. If possible, invite a famous person to speak to the group.

little town called Nazareth. The people were excited because they'd known Jesus since he was a little boy, and they'd been hearing about all the miraculous things he had done.

Jesus stood up in the synagogue and opened the scroll to the book of Isaiah. He read these words.

Show children the Isaiah 61:1-3a transparency.

Have the children read the first four sentences aloud.

SAY Jesus closed the scroll and sat down. All the people watched him very closely.

ASK • Why do you think the people watched him so closely?

SAY They watched him so closely because they were so interested in what he'd say next. They were sitting on the edge of their chairs.

ASK • Why do you suppose Jesus read this passage from Isaiah?

SAY Let's find out what the Bible says. Jesus read the passage from Isaiah, then he said, "The words I just read came true as I spoke. I am the one Isaiah is talking about."

When the people heard this, they were amazed. Jesus was saying that he was the promised one that Isaiah had written about seven hundred years earlier. He was the Savior, the Messiah, the one who would heal the blind and set the prisoners free. He was the one who'd help those who'd been treated unfairly.

ASK • What do you think the people did when they heard what Jesus had to say?

SAY People were so excited they began to whisper about Jesus. They probably whispered, "That's amazing!" "Can you believe that he's Joseph the carpenter's son?" and "Didn't he grow up here in Nazareth?"

ASK • How would you have reacted to Jesus' words?

SAY The people in Nazareth were very familiar with Isaiah's writings. They'd been watching for the Messiah for hundreds of years along with all the other Jews. When Jesus said he was the one Isaiah was talking about, they knew he was saying that he was the Messiah—the one who would be their Savior. He was saying he was the one who would help hurting people everywhere. Let's learn more about how Jesus helps hurting people.

✳ Tears of Sadness

You'll need teardrop shapes of blue tissue paper. They don't need to be more than about three inches tall. Be sure to use the kind of tissue paper that will bleed when it gets wet, which is often available through school supply stores or art supply stores. If you have time, have the children cut out the shapes. Otherwise, prepare three or four for each child ahead of time.

SAY Think about the people you know who are sad and hurting. I'm going to pass out some tissue-paper teardrops. The teardrops represent the tears we cry when we're sad. They're made of blue paper because we say that people are feeling blue when they're sad. On each one, lightly draw a symbol or write a word that'll represent a person you're thinking of. When you finish your shapes, come to the front of the room, and tape them to the mural I've set up.

(continued on page 95)

Worship Leader Tip

Be sure to protect the floor under the mural. Also, make the mural paper at least two or three layers thick to protect the wall from the tissue-paper dye.

Preschool Activities 8

Jesus Teaches in a Synagogue Luke 4:14-21

Worship Theme: Jesus helps hurting people.

Using Theo

Consider using Theophilus the FaithRetriever puppet today in these ways:

- Have Theo lead the preschoolers from the main worship area to the preschool room.
- Invent a sad story for Theo, and ask children to comfort him during "Helping Others' Hurts."
- See the KidsOwn Worship Kit for a puppet skit written for today's worship session.

Helping Others' Hurts

You'll need several stuffed animals, as well as blankets and a first-aid kit or a toy doctor's kit. Invent ailments and stories about why an animal is sad, then assign an ailment or story to each stuffed animal.

Talk to the children about what's wrong with each stuffed animal. Point out the blankets and the first-aid kit, and encourage the children to decide how to comfort each stuffed animal.

ASK • How do you think Jesus would help this stuffed animal?

Allow the children to help the stuffed animals by offering comforting words, by hugging the stuffed animals, or by putting band-aids on them.

ASK • When have you been hurt?
- How does Jesus help you when you're hurt?
- When have you been sad?
- How does Jesus help you when you're sad?

Choose one child to pretend to be Jesus. Have "Jesus" do something to help a classmate who pretends to be hurting. The child pretending to be Jesus might give a hug or a pat on the shoulder. Have the children take turns pretending to be Jesus.

ASK • Why does Jesus help hurting people?

SAY Jesus helps hurting people because he loves them. Jesus loves each one of us, too. Let's say "thank you" to Jesus for helping hurting people and for loving us.

Say "Thank you, Jesus!" with the children.

Jesus Came to Help

Open your Bible to Luke 4:14-22.

SAY Today our Bible story is about a time Jesus went to a synagogue. A synagogue is like a church where Jewish people go to worship God.

Let's pretend that we're at the synagogue on the day the Bible story tells about. Jesus had been going to different synagogues all over, and when people heard what he had to say, they were excited. They liked what Jesus said.

ASK • What would you think if Jesus came to our church today?
- Would you do anything special to get ready for him?

SAY The people were excited when they saw Jesus at their synagogue. Then Jesus got up to speak.

I'll need your help to explain what Jesus told the people. Are you ready? Here we go.

Jesus opened the big Bible scroll, and he read these words.

He said, "The Lord has put his Spirit in me. God has chosen me to tell the good news to poor people."

Let's show what Jesus came to do by telling each other the good news.

(continued on page 94)

(continued from page 93)

Have the children say "Good news! Good news!" to each other child.

SAY Then Jesus read more from the big Bible scroll. He said, "God sent me to tell prisoners that they are free."

Let's show what Jesus came to do by telling prisoners they're free.

Choose one child to pretend to be Jesus. Have the other children crawl under a table, which will represent the jail. Have the child pretending to be Jesus tell the prisoner children that they're free to go. Have the children crawl out from under the table and dance around the room. Choose another child to pretend to be Jesus, and play again. Then have the children sit down on the floor again.

SAY Then Jesus read something else from the big Bible scroll. He said, "God sent me to tell blind people that they can see again."

Let's show what Jesus came to do by telling blind people that they can see.

Choose one child to pretend to be Jesus. Have the other children pretend to be blind by closing their eyes and feeling their way around the room—make sure there are no obstacles they can run into or stumble over. Have "Jesus" put a hand on each child's shoulder and say, "You can see." Have that child open his or her eyes and jump for joy. When all the children have opened their eyes, have them sit down on the floor again.

SAY Then Jesus read something else from the big Bible scroll. He said, "God sent me to help people who've been treated unfairly."

Let's show what Jesus came to do by helping people who've been treated unfairly.

ASK • Have you ever been treated unfairly?
• How did that make you feel?

Have the children cross their arms and pout to show they feel upset about being treated unfairly. Choose one child to pretend to be Jesus. Have that child pat each child on the shoulder and say, "It's OK." Have the child uncross his or her arms and smile. Continue until "Jesus" has helped all the children. Then have the children sit on the floor again.

SAY Then Jesus read one more thing from the big Bible scroll. He said, "God sent me to announce the time God will show his kindness."

Let's show what Jesus came to do by announcing the time God will show his kindness.

Have the children all cup their hands around their mouths and call out, "God is showing his kindness."

SAY Then Jesus closed the scroll and sat down. The people were amazed by what Jesus had said. They said good things about Jesus.

Let's all say good things about Jesus.

Have the children call out, "Jesus came to help people," "Jesus loves us," and "Jesus helps us when we're sad."

Frowns to Smiles

You'll need a white paper plate for each child. You'll also need washable markers, two-prong paper fasteners, and six-inch lengths of yarn.

Encourage the children to draw eyes and a nose on the paper plate, but tell them not to draw a mouth. You'll want to give specific instructions to young preschoolers, such as, "Draw two eyes. Where do you think the eyes should go?"

Tie the yarn to the paper fasteners. Show the children how to press the paper fasteners through the paper plates to form the corners of the mouths. Help them bend back the prongs. (If you have young preschoolers, poke holes in the paper plate where the paper fasteners should go.)

ASK • What does your face look like when you're sad.

Show the children how to bend the yarn into a frown.

ASK • What does your face look like when you're happy?

Show the children how to bend the yarn into a smile.

SAY Jesus helps hurting people. He helps sad, frowning people be happy, smiley people.

(continued from page 92)

Pass out the tissue-paper teardrops and pencils. Give the children four or five minutes to write on the teardrops and tape them to the mural. When all the shapes are on the mural, collect the pencils, and regain the children's attention.

SAY This mural is called the wailing wall. It represents all the people we know who are sad and hurting. Look at this wall, and think about the people who are represented by each teardrop.

ASK • How do you think Jesus feels about our wailing wall and all these hurting people?

SAY Sometimes when we feel sad, we feel like we're all alone. But look at this wall. It shows that there are many, many people who feel hurt, sad, or lonely. The Bible says to be happy with those who are happy and to be sad with those who are sad. Let's be sad with those who are sad today—let's cry along with them.

Invite the children to each spray water from a spray bottle onto the wailing wall and imagine that they're crying along with the sad people represented by the teardrops. Note how the blue from the tissue paper runs onto the mural paper. Say something like, "Look how their sadness is leaking out when we cry along with these sad people."

ASK • What did you think when you saw the blue dye coming out of the teardrops?
• How do you feel when you're sad and someone hugs you, talks to you, or cries with you?

SAY The Bible tells us that when Jesus lived on earth, he cried with his friends when they were sad. When people cry with us, we feel comforted, and a little of our sadness goes away. Jesus understands when we're sad. Jesus helps hurting people, and he offers us comfort and peace. Let's learn more about the help and comfort Jesus gives to hurting people.

✳ Sharing Comfort

SAY The Bible praises God for giving us comfort. Listen to what the Bible says. "Praise be to God...who comforts us in all our troubles so that we can comfort those in any trouble with the comfort we ourselves have received from God...Through Christ our comfort overflows" (2 Corinthians 1:3-5).

ASK • Why do you think Jesus helps hurting people?
• According to the verse I read, what is it we're supposed to do?
• Why is it good for us to comfort others with the comfort that we get from Jesus?
• What do you think it means when it says, "Through Christ our comfort overflows"?

SAY Let's see how overflowing comfort works. First, everyone needs to think of a comforting thing that Jesus might say to someone who is hurting. I'll give you a moment to think. Pause. OK, now that you've got a comforting thought in mind, I'll pick someone to go first. It's that person's job to start spreading his or her message of comfort through the room by saying the comforting words to other people, one at a time. As soon as someone has shared a comforting message with you, it's your job to start spreading your own message of comfort through the room. Keep spreading comfort until I tell you to stop.

Choose a child to begin. Have the children continue sharing comforting words until you see that all the children are involved in sharing comfort. Then regain the children's attention.

ASK
- How did it feel to share comfort with others?
- How did it feel when others shared comfort with you?
- Now what do you think overflowing comfort is?
- How do you think Jesus uses us to help hurting people?

SAY Jesus helps hurting people. He offers them help for their troubles, and he comforts them when they're sad and lonely. The Bible tells us that we have a role too. We can help by sharing the comfort Jesus gives us with others.

Let's Pray!

The Offering

While you take the offering, have the children ask Jesus to use the offering money to help hurting people. Play the song "My God Is" while you take the offering.

Teardrop Prayers

SAY Think of the people you made teardrops for. Let's pray for them, asking Jesus to help them.

Have the children silently pray for the people they made teardrops for. If preschoolers did not make teardrops, ask them to think of someone who is sad and pray for that person.

If the teardrops aren't too wet, cut apart the mural, and have each child take a teardrop or two home as a reminder to ask God to help hurting people.

Sorrow Into Dancing

SAY The Bible says that God turns our sorrow into dancing.

ASK
- What other good things might God turn your sorrow into?

SAY Jesus helps hurting people. Jesus might turn your sorrow into joy or laughter or happiness. Let's sing "Joy!" as a way of praising Jesus for helping us when we're sad and hurting. While you're singing, think about how great Jesus is for helping us.

Sing "Joy!"
Lyrics and motions are in the back of this book.

Jesus Is Rejected in His Hometown

Luke 4:22-30

Worship Theme: Jesus is for everyone.

A Look at the Session

Session Sequence	What Children Will Do	Supplies
Getting Started	Welcome the children to children's church.	**KidsOwn Worship Kit:** *Songs From FaithWeaver, Vol. 6* **Classroom Supplies:** CD player
1 Let's Praise God! (up to 25 minutes)	**Sing:** • "Jesus Is Lord of All" (track 9) • "Joy!" (track 5) • "We Want to See Jesus Lifted High" (track 19) • "Rise Up and Praise Him" (track 14) • "I Love You, Lord" (track 18) • "We Believe in God" (track 10)	**KidsOwn Worship Kit:** *Songs From FaithWeaver, Vol. 6;* Lyrics Transparencies **Classroom Supplies:** CD player, overhead projector, magazines, scissors, newsprint, marker

2 Let's Learn the Point! — PRESCHOOL ACTIVITIES (up to 25 minutes)

What Children Will Do	Supplies
One for Everyone—Play a game to see what it means that Jesus is for everyone.	**Classroom Supplies:** Stuffed animals, small toys, copies of "Jesus Is for Everyone" (p. 107), scissors
Jesus Goes to the Synagogue—Hear the Bible story, and play a game about sharing.	**Classroom Supplies:** Pictures from "One for Everyone"
Jesus Is for Everyone—Decorate pictures of Jesus to give to others.	**Classroom Supplies:** Copies of "Jesus Is for Everyone," crayons, children's scissors

2 Let's Learn the Point! — ELEMENTARY ACTIVITIES (up to 25 minutes)

What Children Will Do	Supplies
✳ **He Is Really God**—Watch a video, and talk about how to know that Jesus is really God.	**KidsOwn Worship Kit:** *KidsOwn Worship Video:* "He Is Really God" **Classroom Supplies:** TV, VCR
✳ **Agree or Disagree**—Listen to "Jesus" and agree or disagree.	**Classroom Supplies:** Index cards, markers, butcher paper, cardboard tubes, script (p. 102)
✳ **For All the World**—Come up with a skit to tell the world that Jesus is for everyone.	**Classroom Supplies:** Bibles, paper, pencils, art supplies

Session Sequence	What Children Will Do	Supplies
3 Let's Pray! (up to 10 minutes)	**The Offering**—Donate the offering to a missionary organization that spreads the gospel.	**Classroom Supplies:** Offering bowls
	Who We Are—Explore who they are and praise God for sending Jesus to everyone.	
	We All Need Jesus—Sing "We Believe in God" as a prayer.	**KidsOwn Worship Kit:** *Songs From FaithWeaver, Vol. 6;* "We Believe in God" (track 10) **Classroom Supplies:** CD player

✳ Starred activities can be used successfully with preschool and elementary children together.

Customize your session to fit your needs. You can separate preschoolers and elementary children for Section 2.

Or, if you keep the children all together for the entire worship session, we suggest you choose from the starred activities.

Why We Worship

The Bible tells us that God loved the world so much that he gave his one and only Son, so that anyone who believes in him can spend eternity with God. The Bible also says that it doesn't matter what country we're from, what our position in life is, or what our gender is. God's offers salvation to all people. Could there be a better reason to worship God?

Skits and Puppets

In the KidsOwn Worship Kit, you'll find a collection of skits titled, "KidsOwn Worship Skits." The skits are designed to be used with Theophilus the FaithRetriever puppet during the preschool activities. You can purchase a Theo puppet at your local Christian bookstore.

Bible Background

Luke 4:22-30

In this passage, Jesus continued the commentary on the passage from Isaiah 61:1-2 he had read. Though identifying himself as the Messiah probably upset his listeners, his further teaching made them furious.

Jesus had sensed and probably heard that the people doubted that he was the Messiah. Before they would believe, they demanded that he perform miracles as he had in Capernaum. In his reprimand for their unbelief, Jesus referred to incidents involving two of the most highly revered Jewish prophets: Elijah and Elisha. He pointed out that God sent Elijah to perform a miracle for a non-Jewish widow in Zarephath, a wicked city where idol worship was practiced. Jesus also mentioned that Elisha healed the leprosy of a Syrian named Naaman but he never healed any of the lepers in Israel. In doing this, Jesus was comparing the people of his hometown to the faithless Jews during the time of Elijah and Elisha. This comparison angered the people, but even more offensive to their culture was the suggestion that non-Jews could enjoy the blessings of God.

In their anger, the people from the synagogue arose and drove Jesus out of town. They no doubt assumed Jesus was guilty of blasphemy—of falsely claiming to be the Messiah. Though it was the Sabbath, when an execution would have been unlawful, it appears they intended to kill Jesus by throwing him off a cliff. We don't know if Jesus escaped miraculously or simply through his air of authority, but he simply passed through the crowd and walked away (Luke 4:30).

 # Getting Started

Before Worship

 Before the worship session, set up a TV and VCR. Cue the *KidsOwn Worship Video* to the segment titled "He Is Really God." Watch the segment at least once before the children arrive so you'll be familiar with it.

Recruit a volunteer to play the part of Jesus for "Agree or Disagree," and have your volunteer wear a Bible-times costume. Photocopy the script on page 102, and go over the script with your volunteer once or twice. Make the script look like a scroll by gluing it onto a length of butcher paper. Glue or tape the ends of the butcher paper to cardboard tubes.

Arrival Time

Play *Songs From FaithWeaver, Vol. 6* as children arrive. Greet children by name, and say to each one, "Welcome to children's church."

 # Let's Praise God!

SAY Hello, everyone! Welcome to children's church. To begin our time together, I'd like all of you to think of a time you felt left out and all alone. I'll give you just a moment to think. Pause.

ASK • How does it feel to be left out and all alone?

SAY At one time or another, every single one of us has felt left out. Feeling left out is no fun. It can make us feel sad, lonely, and discouraged. Today we're going to talk about the fact that Jesus is for everyone. Jesus doesn't leave anyone out—he came for all people. No matter what you look like or how you act, Jesus loves you and wants you to be part of his family. Let's sing.

track 9 Sing "Jesus Is Lord of All."
Lyrics and motions are in the back of this book.

SAY Let's talk about the reasons why people are left out and looked down on.

ASK • When have you seen people being left out? Why were they left out?
• For what reasons do people look down on other people?

SAY Sometimes people are treated badly because of their age or the color of their skin or the country they come from. Sometimes people have a hard time liking those who are different than they are. We call this discrimination. Jesus doesn't want us to discriminate against others. He wants us to be as loving and accepting as he is. Jesus loves everyone, and Jesus wants all people to believe in him and follow him. Jesus is for everyone. While we sing our next song, let's play a game to show that Jesus wants to include everyone. While we're singing, I'll hold someone's waist. Then that person will hold someone else's waist and so on until we make one big chain. Then we'll walk around the room in our great big chain to show that Jesus wants to include everyone.

Song Lyrics and Motions

To make the worship session go more smoothly, tear out the lyrics sheets at the back of this book and keep them in a separate folder. Each week, pull out only the sheets you need for the day's worship session.

 Sing "Joy!"
Lyrics and motions are in the back of this book.

While you're singing "Joy!" put both hands on the waist of a child. Have that child hold another child's waist. Keep going until all the children are linked together in one long chain. Keep walking around the room, holding onto the waist of the person in front of you throughout the entire song. When the song is over, have the children rub both elbows with the person in front of them and behind them and say "Jesus is for you." Then have the children all return to their seats.

SAY **The Old Testament tells us that the Jewish people had been watching and waiting for the Messiah for hundreds of years. When Jesus finally came to live on earth, many Jewish people thought that the Messiah was only for the Jews. Jesus told them that the Messiah was for all people in every country. Many people just didn't understand that. But Jesus wanted all people everywhere to see the truth and know that he is the way to heaven. Let's sing about that.**

 Sing "We Want to See Jesus Lifted High."
Lyrics and motions are in the back of this book.

SAY **Now let's praise Jesus with another song. Let's worship the Holy One with all our heart, with all our soul, and with all our might.**

 Sing "Rise Up and Praise Him."
Lyrics and motions are in the back of this book.

ASK • **Why do you want to praise Jesus today? Why is he worthy of praise and worship?**

SAY **Let's tell Jesus how much we love him.**

 Sing "I Love You, Lord."
Lyrics and motions are in the back of this book.

SAY **Let's make a mural that shows that Jesus is for everyone.**

Provide magazines such as National Geographic (which are often available at used bookstores) or literature from World Vision, Compassion International, or another similar organization. Have the children cut out pictures of people from different cultures. Tape the pictures to the wall under a heading that says "Jesus is for everyone."

SAY **Jesus came for all people in every country around the world. That's because we all need Jesus and the salvation he offers. Jesus wants everyone to believe in him, to love him, and to follow him. Let's sing about believing in Jesus.**

 Sing "We Believe in God."
Lyrics and motions are in the back of this book.

PRAY **God, we do want all in this place to know that you are God, that you are mighty and holy, that you love us, and that we believe in you. God, thank you for sending your Son, Jesus, to the entire world. We know that Jesus is for everyone. Thank you, God. We love you. In Jesus' name, amen.**

For Extra Impact

You may want to invite someone who sponsors a child through World Vision, Compassion International, or another Christian relief agency to talk to the children about telling people from other cultures about Jesus.

Let's Learn the Point!

PRESCHOOL ACTIVITIES, pp. 103–104

At this time, have the preschool helper invite the preschoolers to go to their own room for this section of activities. Tear out the Preschool Activities page, and give it to the preschool leader. Have the preschool leader bring the preschoolers back to participate in the prayer time with the older children. If you prefer to keep all the children together, do the starred activities. They will work well with both elementary and preschool children.

ELEMENTARY ACTIVITIES

* He Is Really God

SAY For hundreds and hundreds of years, the Jewish people had been looking for the special Savior, the Messiah, that God promised to send. Finally Jesus came. But when people listened to what Jesus said, not everyone was sure that Jesus was really the Messiah. Let's watch a video about one person's search for God.

 Watch the video segment titled "He Is Really God." The video shows a secret agent on a special assignment to find out who is really God. After the video segment, ask the following questions.

ASK • How did the secret agent know that Jesus is God?
• How do we know that Jesus is really God—what reasons did you hear in the words to the song?
• Suppose you were alive when Jesus was alive. How would you decide whether Jesus was really the Messiah?
• If you had heard Jesus speak, would you have believed what he said? Why?

SAY The Jews were searching for the Messiah in much the same way the secret agent was in the video we just saw. In the video, the secret agent was convinced that Jesus really was God. When Jesus first began to teach, many people were sure that he really was the Messiah. They believed that the one they'd been waiting for was finally there. Then Jesus said some things these people were not so sure about. Let's find out what happened.

* Agree or Disagree

Hand out index cards and markers. Have the children each write "yes" on one side of their cards and "no way" on the other side. Then have them put the cards on the floor in front of them while they listen.

SAY Today we're going to do some pretending so we can understand how people could be confused about Jesus and his message.

Let's pretend that you are all the people meeting at the synagogue in the town of Nazareth one Sabbath. On this particular day, a man named Jesus is at your synagogue. The Bible tells us that Jesus was just starting his ministry but that news about him had already spread through the whole country. But even if Jesus wasn't well known, you would've known about him because

Jesus grew up in Nazareth—you've known him your entire life.

SAY **Now, in those days, any man who wanted to speak could do so. On this particular day, Jesus wanted to speak to the people—to all of you.** Invite the man you've invited to play the role of Jesus to stand in front of the children. **It will be your job to listen to what Jesus has to say and determine whether you agree** (hold up a "yes" card) **or disagree** (hold up a "no way" card) **with what he says.**

Place a chair next to Jesus. Have Jesus open the scroll prepared before class and read the script, pausing where appropriate. Be sure you have a copy of the script, too.

Jesus: Many years ago, the prophet Isaiah wrote these words. *(Looks at scroll.)* "The Lord's Spirit has come to me, because he has chosen me to tell the good news to the poor. The Lord has sent me to announce freedom for prisoners, to give sight to the blind, to free everyone who suffers, and to say, 'This is the year the Lord has chosen' " *(Luke 4:18-19, Contemporary English Version).*

(Sits down in the chair provided.) Everything you have just heard me read has come true today. I am the one that Isaiah was writing about.

Worship Leader: Children, do you say "yes" or "no way" to what Jesus has just said? *(Pauses for children to hold up their cards.)* When the people in the synagogue heard what Jesus said they were amazed and said good things about Jesus.

Jesus: I know that you've all heard about me. And I know that you will ask me to prove who I am by doing miracles and healing here in my hometown like the miracles and healing I did in the town of Capernaum. But I can tell you that you won't really accept me—prophets are never accepted by those in their own hometown.

Worship Leader: Children, do you say "yes" or "no way" to what Jesus has just said? *(Pauses for children to hold up their cards.)* At this point, I think the people in the synagogue were starting to be a little worried about what Jesus was saying. Let's rub our chins to show we're concerned about what Jesus is saying. *(Rubs chin in a thoughtful manner, saying, "hmmm.")*

Jesus: I tell you the truth. What will happen in these times is the same as what happened in the past. In the days of long ago, there were times when God didn't send his prophets to help the Jews. Instead he sent his prophets to help people who weren't Jewish. He did this because God's people had rejected his ways. You should accept me because I come from God. But you won't fully accept me. I came not only for the Jews, but for the entire world.

Worship Leader: Children, do you say "yes" or "no way" to what Jesus has just said? *(Pauses for children to hold up their cards.)* When the Jews heard Jesus' words this time, they were very angry. Let's show how angry they were by grumbling. *(Helps the children say, "Grumble, grumble, grumble.")*

ASK • **Why do you think they were angry?**

SAY **The Jews believed that they were God's chosen people. They thought they were special and set apart by God. They thought the Messiah was just for them. It made them angry when Jesus said that he was for the entire world. It made them angry because it sounded like Jesus was saying something that was against what everyone accepted as the truth.**

ASK • **What do you suppose the Jews did when they heard what Jesus had to say?**

(continued on page 105)

Preschool Activities

Jesus Is Rejected in His Hometown Luke 4:22-30

Worship Theme: Jesus is for everyone.

Using Theo

Consider using Theophilus the FaithRetriever puppet today in these ways:

• Have Theo lead the preschoolers from the main worship area to the preschool room.

• Have Theo help count the toys and the pictures of Jesus during the "One for Everyone" activity.

• See the KidsOwn Worship Kit for a puppet skit written for today's worship session.

One for Everyone

You'll need lots of stuffed animals and a bucket of small blocks or other small toys so that you have one for each stuffed animal. You'll also need to photocopy the "Jesus Is for Everyone" handout from page 107 and cut out the pictures of Jesus so that you have a picture for every child.

Have the children position the stuffed animals in a line across the room.

SAY In this bucket, I have enough toys for every stuffed animal. But right now, none of the stuffed animals has a toy to play with. We need to make sure that every stuffed animal gets a toy.

Have the children work together to put a small block or toy in front of every stuffed animal. Then go down the row of stuffed animals, and say with the children, "The teddy bear has a toy. The stuffed horse has a toy. The stuffed puppy has a toy." Name each of the stuffed animals to emphasize that every stuffed animal has a toy to play with.

SAY There was a toy in my bucket for every stuffed animal. Now every stuffed animal has a toy.

Play the game again. Gather up the toys, and place them in the bucket. This time, as the children hand out the toys, make sure that they don't give a toy to one or two of the stuffed animals. Then say with the children, "The teddy bear has a toy. The stuffed horse has a toy. The stuffed puppy does not have a toy..." When you get to a stuffed animal that doesn't have a toy, ask, "Is there a toy for this stuffed animal?" Show the children the bucket of toys. When the children indicate that there is a toy for the stuffed animal, say, "Yes, there are toys for all the stuffed animals."

Put the bucket of toys aside.

SAY The Bible tells us that Jesus is for everyone. Just as there were enough toys to go around, there is enough of Jesus to go around.

Have the children line up and sit on the floor. Pass out the pictures of Jesus, saying "One for you; one for you; one for you..."

Then say with the children, "Jesus is for [name of child in the group], Jesus is for [name of another child], Jesus is for [name of another child]" until all the preschool children have been named.

ASK • What does it mean when we say Jesus is for everyone?

SAY It means that Jesus wants to be everyone's friend, and it means that Jesus loves everyone. Jesus is for everyone.

Collect the pictures of Jesus to use in the next activity.

(continued on page 104)

(continued from page 103)

Jesus Goes to the Synagogue

Gather the children.

ASK
- What does it mean to share?
- Is it ever hard to share things with others? Tell us about a time it was hard for you to share.
- How do you feel when others share with you?
- How do you feel when you share with others?

SAY There's a story in the Bible about a time Jesus talked to some people about sharing. Listen while I tell you the story.

One day Jesus went to the synagogue to worship God with the other Jewish people. He told the people that God had sent him to help make sick people feel better and to help sad people not be sad anymore. Then Jesus told them that he wasn't just going to help God's people, the Jews. Jesus said that he was for all people in the world.

This made the Jewish people very angry. They thought that Jesus should only help them. They didn't want to share Jesus with the rest of the world. Let's see what that was like.

Choose two or three children to pretend to be the Jews. Tell everyone else that they are the rest of the people in the world. Give the "Jews" all of the pictures of Jesus.

To the children pretending to be Jews,

SAY Pretend that you want to keep Jesus all to yourself. You don't want to share Jesus with anyone.

To the children pretending to be the rest of the world,

SAY Pretend that you really want to be friends with Jesus. Ask the Jews to share Jesus with you.

Give the children a minute or so to interact. You may need to prompt the children to ask the "Jews" to share Jesus.

SAY The Jewish people didn't understand that Jesus was for everyone. Jesus wanted the Jews to share with the rest of the world. The Bible tells us that Jesus really is for everyone.

Have the "Jews" pass out pictures of Jesus to everyone in the class.

SAY Jesus really is for everyone.

Jesus Is for Everyone

You'll need additional photocopies of the "Jesus Is for Everyone" handout (p. 107). You'll also need crayons or markers and children's scissors.

Give each child several pictures of Jesus. (Older preschoolers will enjoy cutting out the pictures.) Have the children color the pictures.

SAY Jesus is for everyone. You can take these pictures home with you and give them to everyone in your family. You can tell them that Jesus wants to be their friend.

While the children are working, talk about who they'll give the pictures to.

(continued from page 102)

SAY They really respected the laws and teachings about God. And they thought Jesus was being disrespectful of what they knew was right. The Jews in the synagogue were so furious that they got up from where they were worshipping and drove Jesus out of town. They intended to kill Jesus by throwing him off the cliff. But Jesus walked right through the crowd and went on his way.

Jesus: *(Quietly gets up and leaves the room.)*

ASK
• What do you think the Jews thought when Jesus just walked away from them when they were so angry?
• Were the Jews right to be so angry?
• Why couldn't they accept what Jesus was telling them?
• Do you think you would've reacted differently to Jesus than the people in his hometown did? Why or why not?

SAY It's hard to know how we would have reacted to Jesus because we already know so much about him. The Jews were looking for the Messiah, but, when Jesus said things they didn't agree with, it was hard for them to believe that he was the Messiah. Jesus wanted the people to understand that he was the Messiah and that he was for all people.

✳ For All the World

SAY It's easy for us to understand that Jesus is for everyone, but it wasn't all that easy for the Jewish people. For hundreds of years, they'd heard that they were God's special, chosen people. They didn't think that people from other nations were as good as they were. In a way, they were prejudiced against people who weren't Jewish, but they really just didn't understand who Jesus was and who he came for.

Let's pretend that it's our job to convince people all over the world that Jesus is for everyone. In a moment, I'll ask you to form small groups. Then you'll have some time to work together to come up with a way to persuade people that Jesus is for everyone. You can write a song or a poem or a commercial. You can draw a picture or design a mural. You can come up with a game or a dance. It's your choice! You'll have five minutes to put your presentation together.

Have the group form small groups of three or four children. Give each group Bibles, paper, and pencils. Make art supplies available. You may want to direct the children to Scripture passages such as John 3:16-17 and John 16:27.

Give the children five minutes to develop a presentation to show people all over the world that Jesus is for everyone. If you have five or fewer small groups, have each group give its presentation for the rest of the group. If you have more than five small groups, consider having the groups pair up with one other group and present the skits for each other.

ASK
• Why is it a good thing that Jesus is for everyone?
• What would the world be like if Jesus was only for one group of people?
• Why do you think people don't understand that Jesus is for everyone?
• Why is it important that people understand that Jesus is for everyone?

SAY Jesus wants all people to come to him, to love him, and to follow him. Jesus came to save all of us because he loves the entire world. Let's thank Jesus.

 **Let's Pray!** ....

The Offering

Donate this week's offering to a missionary organization that spreads the good news about Jesus to people who've never heard of Jesus. Check with your church office to see if the staff has any literature about the organization that you can show to the children in children's church.

Tell the children about the work the missionary organization does, and explain that this week's offering will go to that group. Explain that the missionaries are telling people all over the world that Jesus is for everyone.

Take the offering.

Who We Are

SAY **People define themselves by lots of different things. You might define yourself by saying that you're from a certain cultural heritage, that you're a certain age, that you go to a certain school, and that you like a certain sport. For example, someone might say that he or she is a Japanese, soccer-loving Christian.**

Think of three things about yourself that define who you are. We'll use them in a prayer in just a moment.

Give the children a moment to think of three things. Then form a circle, and have each child call out three things about himself or herself.

PRAY **God, we are all different in many ways. We like different activities, we look different, we come from different places. But we're the same, too. We all need you. And we know that we are all loved by you. Best of all, we know that Jesus came for each one of us. Thank you, God. In Jesus' name, amen.**

We All Need Jesus

ASK • **Who needs Jesus? If you do, raise your hand.**

SAY **We all need Jesus. Jesus is for everyone. Let's close our time together by singing "We Believe in God" as a prayer.**

 Sing "We Believe in God."
Lyrics and motions are in the back of this book.

Jesus Is for Everyone

Fishermen Are Astonished by a Miraculous Catch

Luke 5:1-11

Worship Theme: Jesus has authority.

A Look at the Session

Session Sequence	What Children Will Do	Supplies
Getting Started	Find a warm welcome at children's church.	**KidsOwn Worship Kit:** *Songs From FaithWeaver, Vol. 6* **Classroom Supplies:** CD player
Let's Praise God! 1 (up to 25 minutes)	Sing: • "Jesus Is Lord of All" (track 9) • "He Is Really God" (track 8) • "Rise Up and Praise Him" (track 14) • "The Good Life" (track 11)	**KidsOwn Worship Kit:** *Songs From FaithWeaver, Vol. 6;* Lyrics Transparencies **Classroom Supplies:** CD player, overhead projector, newsprint, tape, markers, scissors, construction paper

2 Let's Learn the Point! — PRESCHOOL ACTIVITIES (up to 25 minutes)

What Children Will Do	Supplies
Little Fish Story—Learn that Jesus has authority.	**Classroom Supplies:** Fish-shaped crackers, paper cups, bowl, newsprint
Who's in Charge?—Identify some of the things Jesus has authority over.	
Creative Care—Use imagination to experience authority.	

2 Let's Learn the Point! — ELEMENTARY ACTIVITIES (up to 25 minutes)

What Children Will Do	Supplies
✻ **Fishing!**—Learn that Simon Peter put himself under Jesus' authority.	**Classroom Supplies:** Bible, fish-shaped crackers, bowls, straws
✻ **Authority Tag**—Practice obeying authority and see the consequences of ignoring it.	
✻ **Attracted to Authority**—Explore the attraction of Jesus' authority.	**Classroom Supplies:** Tissue paper, scissors, markers, paper, balloons

Session Sequence	What Children Will Do	Supplies
Let's Pray! 3 (up to 10 minutes)	**The Offering**—Offer to follow the Lord as Simon Peter did.	**Classroom Supplies:** Offering bowls
	A New Name—Make name tags that express their commitment to keep a particular commandment.	**Classroom Supplies:** Name tags, markers
	Praise Him—Praise Jesus for his wisdom in using his authority.	**KidsOwn Worship Kit:** *Songs From FaithWeaver, Vol. 6:* "We Want to See Jesus Lifted High" (track 19) **Classroom Supplies:** CD player

✻ Starred activities can be used successfully with preschool and elementary children together.

Customize your session to fit your needs. You can separate preschoolers and elementary children for Section 2.

Or, if you keep the children all together for the entire worship session, we suggest you choose from the starred activities.

Why We Worship

Many people bristle at the word "authority," feeling that somehow anyone in authority is a dominating figure with the right to enforce an indiscriminate set of mandates and to exact punishment for wrongdoing. In the original language of the gospels, however, the word translated as authority meant—in relation to Jesus—delegated influence rather than dominance. That authority includes power but is based on the whole nature of God, not just his power to control. Christ carries the delegated influence of God on earth and in heaven!

Because of Jesus' authority, he can influence the winds and seas, as well as the hearts and minds of human beings. Help your children delight in the knowledge that Jesus can influence them to be all God created them to be when they open their hearts to his authority.

Bible Background

Luke 5:1-11

Simon Peter's initial response to Jesus' command to go fishing stemmed from his experience as a fisherman. Nighttime was the best time to fish—how could Jesus expect to catch fish in broad daylight when the experts had been fishing all night and had caught nothing? Shallow to moderately deep waters were the best places to fish—how could Jesus expect to catch fish in the deep water? Peter shared his doubts, but he didn't hesitate to obey.

The miracle catch of fish dramatically affected Peter. He immediately gained a deeper realization of who Jesus was. Peter was keenly aware of his own sinful inadequacy before the very Lord of the universe and fell at Jesus' feet in worship.

Jesus performed this miracle to demonstrate his power and to help the crowd and the fishermen gain a better understanding of who he was and what was to come. His statement in Luke 5:10 let his followers know that this huge catch of fish was a symbol of what was to come in their evangelistic efforts. For the fishermen-disciples, this was a dramatic, life-changing event. They immediately left their boats and equipment in the hands of their families or hired help and followed Jesus. This was an opportunity they couldn't pass up!

Skits and Puppets

In the KidsOwn Worship Kit, you'll find a collection of skits titled, "KidsOwn Worship Skits." The skits are designed to be used with Theophilus the FaithRetriever puppet during the preschool activities. You can purchase a Theo puppet at your local Christian bookstore.

Song Lyrics and Motions

To make the worship session go more smoothly, tear out the lyrics sheets at the back of this book and keep them in a separate folder. Each week, pull out only the sheets you need for the day's worship session.

Getting Started

Before Worship

Tape a sheet of newsprint to the wall to use during "Let's Praise God!" Cut 1x9-inch strips of construction paper.

For the "Fishing!" activity, set out bowls of fish-shaped crackers on a supply table. You'll need one bowl of crackers for every five children. Make sure that any broken crackers are removed from the bowls—include only whole crackers. Also set out plastic straws and empty bowls. You'll need one straw and one bowl for each child.

For the "Attracted to Authority" activity, inflate balloons, and cut tissue paper into one-inch squares.

Arrival Time

Have *Songs From FaithWeaver, Vol. 6* playing as children arrive. Ask kids to think about all the people who are in charge of them at some time during the week.

Let's Praise God!

SAY **Hello, everyone! As you came in today, I asked you to think about all the people who are in charge of you at some time during the week. Tell me some of the people you thought about.** List the people the children mention on a sheet of newsprint.

ASK • **Why are these people in charge of you?**

SAY **Kids have someone who is in charge to help them make right choices, to teach them, to keep them safe, to protect them, and to care for them. Parents are the final authorities and do all those things for their kids, but your parents delegate, or assign others to do those things, when you aren't together. Your parents trust your teachers, your babysitters, and people like me to do a good job following through with doing what's best for you. Your parents share their authority with others.**

God is like that, too. God is responsible for us, and he cares for us. God sent Jesus to love us, to care for us, and to die for us. The Bible says that God gave Jesus authority over all things. That means that Jesus is in charge. Because Jesus has all authority, he is involved with everything he created, from the wind and the seas to the tiniest sparrow. He's involved with you!

ASK • **What are some big things in your life that Jesus has been involved with?**
• **What are some little things?**

SAY **Jesus is Lord of all those things, the big ones and the small ones. That means that Jesus is in charge, that he's the one in control, that he's the boss. Jesus is involved with everything in your life because he has authority over all the universe—the same kind of loving authority your parents have over you. Jesus is Lord of all. Let's sing about that.**

 Sing "Jesus Is Lord of All."
Lyrics and motions are in the back of this book.

SAY **The song we just sang says that presidents, princes, and paupers will all sing that Jesus is King of kings. That means that Jesus has authority over everybody, rich or poor, powerful or not powerful. Think back to the people you said were in charge of you.** Point to the newsprint list. **Who has authority over them?**

We're going to make chains of command, and you'll each make a chain with a partner. First, look at some of the people you've said have authority, then decide who gave them the authority. Write the names or jobs of people in authority on strips of paper. Then join those strips in a chain, with the highest authority at the top. Some parts of your chain might have more than one link side by side before going down to the next link. Probably, you'll be the last link on the chain, unless you have authority over a pet!

Have the kids pick a partner who is a different age. Make sure each pair has at least one child who can write. Give each pair some strips of construction paper, markers, and access to tape.

Give the children time to do the project. Then let them share their chains with another pair. Walk around, and ask children to share with you who is at the top of their chain.

SAY **I see that lots of you understand that Jesus is at the top of your chain of command. Some of you linked God and Jesus side by side. Jesus has the right to act in God's place because he is really God! He carries the same load that God carries. Jesus has authority from God. Let's sing "He Is Really God."** Encourage the kids to shake their chains as they sing.

 Sing "He Is Really God."
Lyrics and motions are in the back of this book.

SAY **That song says "He holds together everything," like the "Jesus" link holds the rest of your chain. What are some of the things he holds together?**

Wow! If Jesus holds all that together, he deserves our highest praise! We should rise up and praise him! Everyone stand, and let's praise Jesus with this song.

 Sing "Rise Up and Praise Him."
Lyrics and motions are in the back of this book.

SAY **Jesus does deserve our praise and our thanks. He has the authority to care for us and for all creation. He uses his authority to provide for us in big ways and in small ways. He's given us a good life. We need to appreciate the things he's done for us and to honor him for his care. We can do that as we sing "The Good Life."**

 Sing "The Good Life."
Lyrics and motions are in the back of this book.

PRAY **Oh, Lord, you are so great! You have all authority and power over all the earth, and yet you still choose to be with us and to be concerned about everything that happens to us. We worship you today! In Jesus' name, amen.**

Collect the chains and set them aside.

Let's Learn the Point!

PRESCHOOL ACTIVITIES, pp. 113–114

At this time, have the preschool helper invite the preschoolers to go to their own room for this section of activities. Tear out the Preschool Activities page, and give it to the preschool leader. Have the preschool leader bring the preschoolers back to participate in the prayer time with the older children. If you prefer to keep all the children together, do the starred activities. They will work well with both elementary and preschool children.

ELEMENTARY ACTIVITIES

✳ Fishing!

Have children form groups of five. Have each group collect a bowl of fish-shaped crackers, five plastic straws, and five empty bowls from the supply table. Have the children put the bowl of crackers in the middle of the group. Have each child take a straw and an empty bowl. Have the children leave the supplies alone while they listen to your instructions.

SAY We're going to play a game to help us understand today's Bible story. Let's pretend we're all fishermen. It's your job to see how many fish you can get from the bowl in the middle of your group into your own bowl. Here's the catch: You have to use the straw to fish. You'll suck through the straw so that a fish is stuck to the bottom. Then put the fish into your own bowl. The straw should be the only thing that touches the fish—your hands should never touch the fish. You'll have two minutes to see how many fish you can "catch."

Give the children two minutes to catch fish. Then call time.

ASK • How many fish did you catch?
• If you were depending on this method of "fishing," how long do you think you'd have to fish before you'd have enough fish for a meal?
• You only played this game for two minutes. How do you think you'd feel if you played this game all night long and didn't catch a single fish?

SAY The Bible tells about a time Simon Peter and some other fishermen had been fishing all night long. They hadn't caught a single fish.

ASK • How do you think they felt?

SAY I think they were discouraged and tired. The next morning, Jesus came to the lake where the fishermen had been fishing all night long. There was a crowd of people all around Jesus. Jesus climbed into Simon Peter's boat, and they put out a little ways from the shore. Jesus sat down and taught the people from the boat. When Jesus was finished teaching the people, he told Simon Peter to move the boat into deep water and to let down the fishing nets.

Simon Peter said, "But Master, we've worked hard all night and haven't caught anything! But because you say so, we'll let down the nets."

ASK • We've talked about how tired and discouraged Simon Peter was. Why do you think it mattered to him what Jesus said to do?

(continued on page 115)

Preschool Activities 10

Fishermen Are Astonished by a Miraculous Catch Luke 5:1-11

Worship Theme: Jesus has authority.

Using Theo

Consider using Theophilus the FaithRetriever puppet today in these ways:

• Have Theo lead the preschoolers from the main worship area to the preschool room.

• Have Theo shout "Jesus is in charge!" with the children during the "Who's in Charge?" activity.

• See the KidsOwn Worship Kit for a puppet skit written for today's worship session.

Little Fish Story

Before the session, open a big box of fish-shaped crackers and put it where it's accessible but out of sight. Gather the children in a circle. Place a big bowl on some newsprint in the middle of the circle and set out paper cups.

SAY I'm hungry. I think it's time for a snack. I'm going to eat the snack in my cup. Show the empty paper cup. Oh, there's nothing in my cup. I'm going to get a snack from this bowl. Dip your paper cup into the empty bowl.

ASK • Can you see my snack?

SAY I could keep dipping my cup in this bowl all day, and I still wouldn't have a snack, because there's no snack there! This reminds me of a Bible story.

One day Simon Peter, James, and John were fishing. They fished with big nets. Let's all link our arms to make a big net. Have the children wrap their arms around the arms of the people next to them and join hands.

They threw out their nets because they wanted to catch fish, just like I wanted to catch a snack in my cup. Let's count to three and throw our net toward the bowl in the center. Have the children bring their arms up and over the top without dropping hands.

Did you catch anything? Neither did Simon Peter, James, and John. So they did it again. Have the children repeat the action. And again. Say "and again" several times, a little quicker each time so the kids pick up the pace of their "net throwing."

But they still didn't catch anything. So they came back to the shore and started washing their nets. Have children drop hands and pretend to wash their hands.

Then Jesus got into Simon Peter's boat and asked him to put out a little from the shore. So Simon Peter took Jesus out in his boat a little way from the shore. Then Jesus taught the people who were sitting on the shore.

When Jesus was done teaching, he told the fishermen to get their nets (have the children connect their arms again) and try again to catch some fish. Simon Peter said, "We fished all night, and there are no fish! But, because you say so, we'll do it." Are you ready to throw the nets again? This time, close your eyes while we count. One...two...three. On three, empty the package of crackers into the bowl. Allow some to overflow the bowl onto the table.

They caught so many fish that they needed help to bring them in! Help me bring them in. Give each child a cup. Dip your cups into the bowl, and get some fish.

Jesus took care of the fishermen, who caught some fish. The fish came because Jesus wanted them to be there. Jesus showed his authority that day, and the fishermen were ready to follow him anywhere.

Who's In Charge?

ASK • Do you know what it means when someone asks, "Who's in charge, here?"

(continued on page 114)

(continued from page 113)

ASK • Who is in charge at your house? at the library? at church?

SAY Jesus is in charge of everything, everywhere. The Bible tells us that Jesus made everything. Let's take turns around the room naming something that Jesus made. When it's your turn, jump up and tell us something that Jesus made. The rest of us will shout back to you, "Jesus is in charge." I'll start. Jump up. Jesus made the fish in the sea! Encourage the children to shout back, "Jesus is in charge." Allow each child to have a turn.

Since Jesus made everything, Jesus can be in charge of everything. Being in charge is the same thing as having authority. Jesus has authority over each thing on earth, including you and your family. Because he is in charge, he'll take care of you and everything else he made.

Creative Care

For this activity, you can either use clay or have the children pretend to use clay.

ASK • When have you been in charge of something?

SAY Today we're going to play a game where you're in charge. To play this game, you'll have to use your imagination. I have a huge chunk of imaginary clay. I'm going to give a piece to each of you. Are you ready?

Preschool Leader Tip

Preschoolers are full of imagination! Since they have little experience with the responsibility of authority, this game can help them experience what it might be like to be in charge. Your enthusiasm in leading this activity will help them participate fully and get the most out of this experience.

Pretend to lift a large block of clay and carry it around to each child. Have some children pinch off their own clay, and pull off big pieces for others. As you move around, ask questions such as "Is that enough?" or say "That's a lot of clay, mister." Keep the interaction rolling. Put the imaginary clay down, and pinch off a piece for yourself.

SAY There's a lot we can do with this imaginary clay. We can stretch it and roll it. We can toss it up in the air! We can step on it, or make it into a big ball. As you say each thing, pantomime the action and encourage the children to do so. Take a little time with this step.

After you've finished working your clay to make it nice and soft, I want each of you to pretend to make something with it...anything you want! I'm going to give you a minute to work, then you can tell what you've created. Pause to allow children to work. Then ask children to share what they've created.

Now that you've created your things, you are in charge, no matter what happens. Look out! Here comes a giant bird that wants to peck pieces out of your creation! What are you going to do? Show me. Encourage the children to somehow protect their creation.

Whew! You did a great job of being in charge of your creation. Oh no! Here comes a steamroller! It's rolling over the ground, crushing everything in its path. Can you save your creation?

Continue through one or more of the following scenarios. For each, have the children imagine what they would do if they were in charge.

• Your creation is hungry.

• Your creation is growing too big for its clothes.

• Your creation wants to walk on its own.

• Your creation is afraid of the dark.

• Your creation has a broken piece.

SAY It's time to put your creation to bed, so tuck it in, then look at me. Wow! It's a lot of work to be in charge! You did great. Were your creations safe when you got them into bed? Even though lots happened, you kept your creations safe because you had the authority to do whatever was necessary to protect them. You could fight off any enemy and provide for every need your creation had.

ASK • Who has that authority over your life?

SAY The one who created you has the authority to provide fish for your dinner, just as he provided for Simon Peter, James, and John. He has the authority to help you not be afraid of the dark, to help you when you're hurt, to find you when you wander off, to take care of you in every way.

ASK • Since Jesus has that authority, what should we do?

Integrate the answers the children give into the prayer.

PRAY Jesus, thank you for having authority in our lives. Because you do, we trust you, we worship you, we obey you, we honor you. In Jesus' name, amen.

(continued from page 112)

ASK • Do you think Simon Peter had any clue about what was going to happen?
 • Why did Simon Peter obey Jesus?

SAY When Simon Peter and the other fishermen let down the nets this time, they caught so many fish that the nets began to break. They filled up two boats so full that the boats began to sink. Take a big handful of fish crackers to put in your own bowl. You can munch on them while we talk.

ASK • What do you think Simon Peter and the other fishermen thought when they caught so many fish?

SAY Let's see what the Bible says.

Have someone read Luke 5:8-9 aloud.

ASK • Why do you think he fell at Jesus' knees?
 • What would you have done?

Have someone read aloud verses 10 and 11.

ASK • Why were they willing to follow Jesus?
 • Why are you willing to follow Jesus?

SAY Simon Peter and his partners, James and John, saw Jesus' authority over nature. They realized that if Jesus could guide fish into their nets that he could also do other great things. They wanted to be under Jesus' authority. They wanted to be associated with this powerful man. So they followed him. Let's learn more about Jesus' authority.

✳ Authority Tag

Clear an area in the room.

ASK • Have you ever been in a car when a police officer was directing traffic?
 • When the police officer raises his or her hand, what does the driver of the car do?

SAY The officer does not have to physically stop the car. The driver stops because the officer has the *authority* to tell him to stop. The officer's word has enough authority to stop the car.

 Let's do an activity to illustrate what I mean by authority.

Play a form of Freeze Tag in which one child is the "officer" who has the authority to tag the others who must freeze in place. Play a short game.

ASK • Why did you freeze?
 • Why did you choose to obey?

SAY The officer in our game had the authority to freeze you. In this case, authority means the responsibility to command and to enforce laws. In our game, we didn't set up any punishments for not freezing, but what happens if a person chooses to keep going when a police officer says to stop?

 Let's play the game again. This time, you have the freedom to choose not to stop. But there are consequences for choosing not to stop. If you choose not to freeze, you must sit down. Play a short game.

ASK • Are there consequences for not obeying Jesus' directions? What are those consequences?

• Why do you think people can choose whether they're going to obey?

SAY God gave people the responsibility to choose whether to obey him. But, just like in the game we played, there are consequences to disobeying. When we put ourselves under Jesus' authority, we choose to obey him, and Jesus cares for us as his children. Jesus always uses his authority in love and justice. We can trust that his care is so great that he will always be working for our good, just as he did for Simon Peter, James, and John.

✳ Attracted to Authority

Have children choose partners. Give each pair tissue paper squares, a marker, and an inflated balloon.

SAY We're going to use these supplies to explore authority. On each of your squares of tissue paper, write or draw a picture of some created thing. You can be really specific and name a person or title (such as president), or you can be general and name something like wind or soil. Give the kids time to complete your instructions. Then have them scatter their squares of paper over a small area of table top.

Now I want the partners in each pair to rub the balloon on their heads to charge it with static electricity. When your balloon is fully charged, begin to explore what happens as you hold your balloon at different distances from the paper squares. Give the kids several minutes to do the experiment. Each pair will have a somewhat unique experience.

ASK • How is the static electricity in the balloon like authority?

• How is it different?

• How did the tissue respond to the authority of the balloon?

• How is that like the way the things or people written on your squares might respond to Jesus' authority?

SAY The "authority" we gave to the balloon was imperfect, and so your results might have varied from pair to pair. If we had been able to charge the balloon with enough static electricity—given it enough "authority"—every square would have been attracted to it eventually.

God gave Jesus all authority, and his authority is perfect. The Bible tells us that "at the name of Jesus every knee should bow, in heaven and on earth and under the earth." Remember how Simon Peter fell to his knees to show that he was giving himself to Jesus' authority? This verse in Philippians lets us know that eventually everyone will answer to Jesus' authority.

ASK • Why do you think some people respond to Jesus' authority like hard-to-pick-up pieces of paper?

SAY The Bible reminds us of Jesus' words "If you love me, you will obey what I command" (John 14:15).

ASK • Which of Jesus' commands must be obeyed if you choose to be under his authority?

PRAY God, help us jump quickly to your authority like those little squares of tissue paper. Help us to show our love for you by keeping the commandments we know you have the authority to give us. And help us to trust you to care for us through the authority you have over all of creation. In Jesus' name, amen.

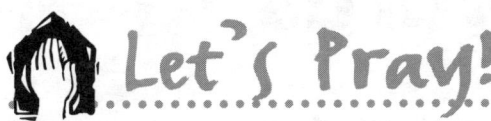 Let's Pray!

The Offering

SAY Let's give our offering as an act of worship. When we give our offering, we are saying that we recognize Jesus' authority over our money and possessions. Bring your offering to the front, and kneel as Simon Peter did at Jesus' feet. Tell Jesus that you know he has authority and you want to put yourself under his authority. Even more than offering our Lord money, we should offer him ourselves.

A New Name

Give each child a name tag and a marker.

SAY A name is something people call us to get our attention. But in the Old Testament and among some other cultures of the world, a name describes what the person is or does. Today, I'm going to ask you to give yourself a name that describes how you see yourself responding to Jesus' authority. For example, you might name yourself simply "Follower of Jesus." If you understand that Jesus is asking you not to fight with your little brother, you might be really specific and call yourself "She who fights no more." Take a minute to think about how you'd like to respond to Jesus' authority today, then write your new name on a name tag. When you're finished, look around to see if there's someone who needs your help writing. If you can't write your own name tag, one of us will help you after you've had a chance to think about it. Walk around, and help children who are having difficulty.

Before you put your name tag on, bow your head, and ask Jesus to help you live up to your new name.

Praise Him

SAY Simon Peter placed himself under Jesus' authority and followed him. Simon Peter trusted Jesus to use his authority wisely and justly. And Jesus does, because he is exactly like God. That deserves our praise!

There are many ways to praise God. We can praise him in song, in prayer, by clapping, or even jumping with joy. As we say, "Praise you, Jesus," feel free to express yourself in different ways—you can whisper, shout, jump, sing, or anything else you can think of.

PRAY Lord, we praise you because you have all authority in heaven and earth and the wisdom to use it. Now, as we say "Praise you, Jesus" together, may you be honored by our worship. Let's all say together, "Praise you, Jesus!" In Jesus' name, amen.

 **track 19** Play "We Want to See Jesus Lifted High."
Lyrics and motions are in the back of this book.

Leader SkillBuilder

When asking questions to help children discover spiritual truths for themselves, the leader often has a specific answer in mind. It can be tempting to dismiss children's answers when they do not match that specific answer. However, by avoiding the temptation to reject an answer, your discussions may become richer and fuller than you thought possible. Often, we can learn a great deal by seeing a truth through another's eyes. Correct errors in theology, but seek to find a nugget of truth in each response.

Jesus Teaches About Rewards

Luke 6:17-26

Worship Theme: Seeking God's kingdom honors him.

A Look at the Session

Session Sequence	What Children Will Do	Supplies
Getting Started	Find a warm welcome at children's church.	**KidsOwn Worship Kit:** *Songs From FaithWeaver, Vol. 6;* Right Angle Viewer **Classroom Supplies:** CD player
Let's Praise God! *(up to 25 minutes)*	**Sing:** • "Joy!" (track 5) • "The Good Life" (track 11) • "Seek Ye First" (track 13) • "Praise, I Will Praise You, Lord" (track 6) • "Love With the Love of Jesus" (track 16)	**KidsOwn Worship Kit:** *Songs From FaithWeaver, Vol. 6;* Lyrics Transparencies; *KidsOwn Worship Video:* "Upside Down" **Classroom Supplies:** CD player, overhead projector, TV, VCR, paper, marker, ruler

2 Let's Learn the Point! PRESCHOOL ACTIVITIES *(up to 25 minutes)*

What Children Will Do	Supplies
Out of the Box—Guess what parts of pictures are, then see the whole picture.	**Classroom Supplies:** Bible, construction paper, scissors, pictures
Kingdom Prayer—Learn a prayer with motions.	
Butterfly Promises—Make caterpillar finger puppets to be reminded to look at things the way God sees them.	**Classroom Supplies:** Pompoms, construction paper, hole punch, white glue, double-sided tape

2 Let's Learn the Point! ELEMENTARY ACTIVITIES *(up to 25 minutes)*

What Children Will Do	Supplies
✱ **Heart Illusions**—Learn that tricks of the world can be very convincing.	**Classroom Supplies:** Bibles, paper, pencils, newsprint, marker
✱ **Treasure Hunt**—Participate in a treasure hunt.	**Classroom Supplies:** Cardboard, chocolate coins, scissors, treasures, label, marker
✱ **Empty Promises**—Make a choice based on appearances and discover the unreliability of the strategy.	**Classroom Supplies:** Empty soda cans, milk carton, water, salt, clear cups

Session Sequence	What Children Will Do	Supplies
Let's Pray! *(up to 10 minutes)*	**The Offering**—Sing a song and offer to place God above everything.	**KidsOwn Worship Kit:** *Songs From FaithWeaver, Vol. 6:* "We Want to See Jesus Lifted High" (track 19) **Classroom Supplies:** CD player, offering bowl
	I Just Seek You—Seek the things of God with a prayer poem.	
	Quiet Reflection—Pray quietly and listen to God.	**KidsOwn Worship Kit:** *Songs From FaithWeaver, Vol. 6:* "Praise, I Will Praise You, Lord" (track 6) **Classroom Supplies:** CD player, candle, match

✱ Starred activities can be used successfully with preschool and elementary children together.

Customize your session to fit your needs. You can separate preschoolers and elementary children for Section 2.

Or, if you keep the children all together for the entire worship session, we suggest you choose from the starred activities.

Why We Worship

We worship a God whose kingdom is based on a different reality than what we see through eyes limited by human perspective. God operates in a realm of eternal perspective. He sees that the things we place a high value on are temporary. Occasionally, we get a glimpse into his line of vision and realize that all we hold dear may not be all there is. In those moments, we experience a bit of God's perspective and are blessed. We can tolerate being poor, sad, or alienated because we know his kingdom is ahead and what lies behind matters less to us.

The world always has and always will give us flawed feedback about who we are and what we are worth. When we see with God's vision, we can let go of the tokens of approval the world offers and follow Jesus with abandon. We worship a God who longs to clear away the tokens of our life and give us himself in abundance. When we seek beyond the treasures of our earthly kingdoms and enter his heavenly one, God is honored.

Bible Background

Luke 6:17-26

Jesus continued to teach and heal people wherever he went. Luke 6:17-26 records a sermon that closely parallels the Beatitudes recorded by Matthew in Jesus' Sermon on the Mount. Some contend that Luke's "Sermon on the Plain" recorded here was the same sermon and that the terrain was described differently because Luke was describing the large plain where the people sat and Matthew was describing the place slightly above the people where Jesus stood on the mountain. Others hold that these were two separate sermons and that Jesus may have spoken similar content numerous times in his ministry.

Jesus' sermon was addressed to his disciples, not to the entire crowd (Luke 6:20). The disciples mentioned here were not just the Twelve, but rather a large crowd, as described in Luke 6:17. A greater multitude also gathered behind the disciples and listened, perhaps on the way to becoming disciples.

Jews listening to Jesus' teaching in this passage would have quickly connected this teaching method with that of the prophets. The prophets had pronounced blessing on appropriate behavior and woe on disobedience. *Blessed,* often translated *happy,* means to have an inner quality of life that demonstrates joy and blessing. *Woe* indicates deep pain or disappointment and conveys a feeling of desperation.

In these Beatitudes Jesus offers hope to those who suffer: a kingdom for the poor, satisfaction for the hungry, laughter for the weeping, and rewards for those suffering for Jesus. For those who put him first and seek his kingdom, all these things will be added.

The woes Jesus enumerates are opposites of the blessings he lists, but this doesn't mean that it is inherently wrong to have enough money, to be well fed, to laugh, or to be well thought of. Instead, Jesus is pointing out that those living "the good life" may find it easy to ignore God and to depend on themselves rather than on him.

Skits and Puppets

In the KidsOwn Worship Kit, you'll find a collection of skits titled, "KidsOwn Worship Skits." The skits are designed to be used with Theophilus the FaithRetriever puppet during the preschool activities. You can purchase a Theo puppet at your local Christian bookstore.

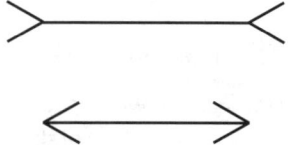

Song Lyrics and Motions

To make the worship session go more smoothly, tear out the lyrics sheets at the back of this book and keep them in a separate folder. Each week, pull out only the sheets you need for the day's worship session.

Getting Started

Before Worship

Set up a TV and VCR, and cue the *KidsOwn Worship Video* to the "Upside Down" segment. Watch the segment at least once before the worship session so you'll be familiar with it.

Use a black marker and ruler to draw two identical lines on two separate pieces of paper. Draw diagonal lines toward the center at each end of one line, making a two-sided arrow. Draw diagonal lines away from the line at each end of the other line, creating an inverse arrow. (See diagram.) Put the two papers where they will be available during Let's Praise God!

For the "Treasure Hunt" activity, buy chocolate coins. Carefully open the foil coverings and remove the chocolate. Replace the chocolate with cardboard of the same thickness. Replace the foil around the cardboard, and hide the cardboard coins somewhere in the room.

Set up a refreshment station. Place a carton of milk, an empty soda can, a soda can filled with water, and a soda can filled with salt on the table. Make sure each can is a different type of soda and the cans look as untouched as possible.

Arrival Time

Have *Songs From FaithWeaver, Vol. 6* playing as the children arrive. Greet children by name, look through the Right Angle Viewer from the KidsOwn Worship Kit, and say, "I'm seeking God's kingdom, but I'm having trouble finding it. Would you like to have a look?" Let some of the kids look into the Right Angle Viewer.

Let's Praise God!

SAY Hello, everyone! Today we're going to talk about looking for, or *seeking,* God's kingdom. Let's talk about what happened when you looked through the Right Angle Viewer.

ASK • What did you see when you looked through the viewer?
• Were you surprised by what you saw when you looked through the viewer? Why or why not?

SAY Today we're going to talk about seeking God's kingdom. We're going to discover that things aren't always what they seem and that you can't always trust the messages that come from society and the world. Those messages can lead us off track just as looking through this Right Angle Viewer would cause us to bump into things.

We're going to find out that God is pleased and honored when we look past the false messages the world sends us and give our whole hearts to seeking his kingdom.

God's kingdom is more than a place—heaven. It's a way of living that honors God and sees the world through God's eyes. God's way of seeing and doing things—his kingdom—is full of love, joy, and light. Let's sing a song that helps us claim the gifts of his kingdom.

 **track 5** Sing "Joy!"
Lyrics and motions are in the back of this book.

ASK • What are some of the things that people look for to bring them love or joy?
• Do those things make people happy?
• Sometimes those things do make people feel happy for a while. But do you think that those things alone will make people happy forever?

SAY People say they want *the good life*. They usually mean they want more stuff—money, toys, newer houses, or the right kind of clothes.

ASK • Who do you think is impressed by stuff?
• How do you think God's idea of the good life is different from people's?

SAY See if you get any more ideas from the next song.

 **track 11** Sing "The Good Life."
Lyrics and motions are in the back of this book.

ASK • What are some of the good things listed in the song?

SAY God wants us to seek him first. That means we need to try to see God's point of view before we decide what *we* want. It's kind of like this: if I asked you to pick out any treat you wanted, how many of you would choose a vegetable? Raise your hands. How about a meat? How about something sweet and full of sugar? Have the kids raise their hands for each choice.

ASK • What would happen if you spent all your time and energy working really hard to get that sugary treat without ever eating what is best for you?

SAY Now, God's kingdom isn't boring like some people think vegetables and meat are. But it *is* what's best for us, like healthy food is best for our bodies. When people eat only sugary treats, they feel tired and depressed, and they get sick. When people eat healthy foods, they feel good, and they are strong and healthy.

Seeking God's kingdom—God's way—is similar. If we waste all our energy on getting what we want, or what the world tells us is good, we'll be unhappy; we won't live good, productive lives. God wants us to seek his kingdom first. When we do things God's way instead of the world's way, God is honored, and we have the best life we could ever hope to live.

That's the message of the next song we're going to sing. The song comes right out of the Bible, from Matthew 6:33. It's called "Seek Ye First." Remember that the word "ye" is another form of the word you, and this song has a message for each of us.

 **track 13** Sing "Seek Ye First."
Lyrics and motions are in the back of this book.

SAY That song reminds us of God's promise that if we seek the kingdom of God first, we will find all that we need. That way of doing things—not worrying about what *we* want or need—doesn't make much sense to those who don't know Jesus as a loving, caring Savior who wants the best for his children. That kind of thinking seems a little upside down.

 Show the video segment titled "Upside Down."

ASK • What was this video about?

• What does the world think is important?

• What does God think is important?

• Why do you think God's values are so different from the world's values?

SAY By the world's standards, God's way of doing things is upside down. But God sees what's real and what's not.

Here's an example of how the world thinks. Use your imagination a little. Imagine that these figures represent God's blessing. I'm going to give one to [child's name]. Give the drawing with the arrows pointing out to the child, and have him or her hold it up so that everyone can see it. **This blessing means that** [child's name] **lives in a really big house and has pretty much whatever toys** [he or she] **wants. I'm going to give *this* blessing to** [second child's name]. Hand the drawing with the arrows pointing in to the second child, and have him or her hold it up.

ASK • If that one means a lot of blessing—a lot of stuff—what do you think this one means?

SAY The first arrow looks longer than the second arrow. So, by the looks of things, the first person has lots of God's blessing, and the second person has not so much, right? But let's find out what's really here. Ask a third child to come up and measure the lines.

ASK • Which line was longer?

• Who has the most blessings?

SAY Sometimes what we think we see isn't really what's there. It looked like the first arrow was longer. But it wasn't. Sometimes it might seem that people with lots of stuff have lots of blessings. But when you measure things according to God's standards, you see that God cares more about how we act and think than he does about how much stuff we have.

 Sing "Praise, I Will Praise You, Lord."
Lyrics and motions are in the back of this book.

SAY One of the biggest upside-down things about God's kingdom is his love. The world says we should only love people who look nice, act nice, and have nice things. Or maybe the world tells us we should love people who are just like us. But God's kingdom is different. God says we are to love people who are grumpy, mean to us, and different from us. That's upside down!

ASK • How can we love the way God says to love?

SAY The only way to love as God says to is to seek God's kingdom—or God's attitudes—first. Then we can love with the love that can only be Jesus.

 Sing "Love With the Love of Jesus."
Lyrics and hand motions are in the back of this book.

PRAY God, we want to honor you by seeking your kingdom. We want to see with your eyes and love with your love. In Jesus' name, amen.

Let's Learn the Point!

PRESCHOOL ACTIVITIES, pp. 125–126

At this time, have the preschool helper invite the preschoolers to go to their own room for this section of activities. Tear out the Preschool Activities page and give it to the preschool leader. Have the preschool leader bring the preschoolers back to participate in the prayer time with the older children. If you prefer to keep all the children together, do the starred activities. They will work well with both elementary and preschool children. ● ● ● ● ● ● ● ● ● ● ➤

ELEMENTARY ACTIVITIES

✳ Heart Illusions

SAY During our praise time, we looked at an optical illusion. We saw two lines with arrows drawn at the ends. One line looked longer than the other. But we found out that both lines were the same length. We call things like that optical illusions because they fool our eyes. The word "optical" means having to do with our eyes.

ASK • Can you think of some other optical illusions you've seen?

SAY Many tricks fool our eyes. Some tricks fool our ears. Some tricks fool our minds. Let's try one of those right now. Pick a partner. If you're pretty good at math, please choose someone who may not yet know how to do all that you can. For example, a fifth grader might be able to help a first-grade partner. Give each pair a pencil and a piece of paper.

Here are your instructions.

Write down any two numbers between 50 and 100.
Add the two numbers together.
Looking at your total, cross out the digit that's farthest to the left.
Add one to the number.
Subtract that number from the total of the first two numbers you added.
Everyone's answer, if done correctly, will be ninety-nine (see diagram).

Compare your number with three other pairs.

ASK • What did you discover?

SAY That's a mind trick based on math facts. It's really kind of fun. But there's another kind of trick, or illusion, that isn't funny at all. It's a heart trick. Heart tricks are the things the world tells you are important, when really they're not.

ASK • What are some things the world tries to trick you into believing?

Encourage kids to look up Luke 6:17-26 to start the list. Write their answers on newsprint or a chalkboard.

ASK • What are some ways we can keep from being fooled by the heart illusions the world wants us to believe?

SAY The things you just mentioned—things like reading the Bible, praying, talking to people you trust—those are all ways to seek God's kingdom. God is honored when we take the time to ask him what's real and to seek his kingdom.

Worship Leader Tip

This activity is one of the few opportunities your mathematically gifted students may have to shine in a church setting. Allow a child who is finding this challenge easy to help others who may be having a more difficult time with the calculations required for this activity.

If you have a group of young children, do this activity together on the chalkboard or newsprint. Complete the exercise several times with different children contributing each time around. Do it until your kids see the answer will always be ninety-nine.

$$\begin{array}{r} 76 \\ +87 \\ \hline \cancel{1}63 \end{array}$$

$$\begin{array}{r} 63 \\ +\ 1 \\ \hline 64 \end{array}$$

$$\begin{array}{r} 163 \\ -64 \\ \hline 99 \end{array}$$

When doing a large group
activity, such as a treasure
hunt, plan creative crowd-
control methods. Make sure
there are enough items to
engage the interest of the
entire group. Break large
groups into smaller groups,
and assign adult leaders to
each group if necessary. Set
a time limit, and stick to it.
Offer noise-level guidelines,
such as using "inside voices."
Planning ahead, based on
your understanding of your
particular group of children,
helps you avoid pitfalls and
have an enjoyable and
meaningful activity.

Worship Leader Tip

By this point in the lesson,
some of your kids may
anticipate the outcome of
this activity. If some of them
make correct assumptions,
you can affirm their wisdom
in the discussion time with
comments such as "I see
you are looking beyond the
obvious. That's a good step
in seeking God's kingdom."

* Treasure Hunt

Before the session, hide the cardboard gold coins and several other "treasures" in the room. One of the items should be labeled, "The Kingdom of God." Other items should represent what people tend to seek instead of the kingdom of God.

Have the children form teams of five.

SAY Let's have a treasure hunt. This treasure hunt is a little different than most treasure hunts. There are many things hidden in this room that could be the treasure. The key is to discover what the real treasure is. When your team finds what you think is the real treasure, raise your hand and tell us what it is. After each team has found the treasures, we'll decide what the real treasure is.

ASK • What does it mean to *seek* things of this world?
• What kinds of things does the world treasure?
• Why do you think people treasure those things?
• What do they think those things will bring them?
• What does God want us to treasure?

SAY We need food, money, clothes, and shelter, but we're not told to seek those things. We're told to seek the kingdom of God. In that way, we bring honor to God by placing him above everything else. The wonderful thing is that, as we seek the kingdom of God, God provides all those other things we need as well.

* Empty Promises

Have children form groups of four. Point to the beverage containers.

SAY In your group, decide which beverage your group would most like to drink. You can discuss the advantages of each and appoint a representative to come and tell me your decision.

As children report their choices, ask kids representing different beverage choices to remain with you. One at a time, have those who chose soda pour from the can they selected into a cup. Invite them to "drink" what's been poured. After contents have been poured from all the cans, lead the children in the following discussion.

ASK • How do you feel about what's in the container your group chose?
• What information did you use to make your decision?
• What information did you really need to make a good decision?

SAY On the outside, each can of soda promised something good and sweet, but it was an empty promise. The promise wasn't backed up by the contents.

ASK • Have you ever bought something that you wanted really badly only to find that it wasn't as good as you expected? If so, raise your hand.
• Have you ever done something that you thought was a good idea at the time but that ended up getting you in trouble? If so, raise your hand.

SAY Jesus wanted the people to know that they needed to be careful when they decided what kinds of things to pursue. Jesus knew that it's really easy to get excited by things that look good but that really aren't good. Sometimes people try to get things that they think will make them happy, such as money, toys, or vacations. But those things won't really make us feel happy or satisfied. That's why Jesus told the people to seek God's kingdom above all other things. Seeking God's kingdom will make us truly happy, and it also honors God.

(continued on page 127)

Preschool Activities

Jesus Teaches About Rewards Luke 6:17-26

Worship Theme: Seeking God's kingdom honors him.

Using Theo

Consider using Theophilus the FaithRetriever puppet today in these ways:

• Have Theo lead the preschoolers from the main worship area to the preschool room.

• Have Theo sniff the caterpillar. Tell Theo it will be a butterfly, and let him struggle with how that could possibly be, since it doesn't look, smell, or act like a butterfly.

• See the KidsOwn Worship Kit for a puppet skit written for today's worship session.

Out of the Box

Before the worship session, cut a two-inch square out of the center of a dark piece of paper. Discard the small square, and keep the large piece of paper with the window in it. You'll hold this paper over various magazine or calendar pictures so that a small area of the picture is revealed. Choose pictures that show interesting visual details through the window without revealing what the picture is. Open your Bible to Luke 6:17-26.

SAY In our Bible story today, Jesus talked about how things aren't always as they seem. He said that people who really wanted to be with him were happy, and that people who seemed to have everything they wanted might be sad. He said that people who have lots of friends might not

be friends with God. He said that people who look rich might really be poor because they don't know God.

I have some pictures to show you. They'll help us understand how things aren't always as they seem.

Show the pictures one at a time through the construction-paper window . Ask the children to guess what each picture is based on what they can see. Then reveal the whole picture so they can see it.

ASK • What happened when we couldn't see the whole picture?

SAY We don't always understand all about things that happen to us. We understand little bits, like the little bit of each picture we could see.

ASK • Who can always see the whole picture, even the parts we can't see?

SAY God really likes it when we ask him what he sees. That's what the Bible calls seeking God's kingdom. We can ask God to help us think about things the way he thinks about them. Let's learn a prayer to help us seek God's kingdom.

Kingdom Prayer

Gather the children in a circle. Help the children learn the words and motions for this prayer.

Dear God, help me
See what you see,

(Raise both pointer fingers, and touch them to your eyes, then to each other at chest level.)

(continued on page 126)

(continued from page 125)

Hear what you hear,	(Raise your pointer and middle fingers, and touch them to your ears, then to each other at chest level.)
Think what you think,	(Raise your pointer, middle, and ring fingers. Touch them to your temples, then to each other at chest level.)
And feel what you feel.	(Raise all fingers. Cross your hands over your heart, then touch fingers of both hands together to form a peak and touch each other at chest level.)
In Jesus' name, amen.	(Keep the peak, and bring palms together in a clap.)

Butterfly Promises

Use a hole punch to punch circles from construction paper. Put two tiny dots of white glue on a pompom and attach the paper circles as eyes. Put a piece of double-sided tape on the bottom of the pompom, and stick it to the fingernail of your index finger.

Have the kids all watch to see what happens. Creep your finger up your chest and on to your shoulder, where you will have a conversation with the finger puppet. Occasionally lift your finger to let the "caterpillar" look around.

ASK
• What's this little fellow?
• What can you tell me about caterpillars?

SAY Boy, if you just looked at him, you'd never know he had much of a future. But God has a plan. God sees this little guy differently than we do.

Little caterpillar, are you rich? Have the puppet whisper in your ear. **He doesn't feel rich! He feels kind of poor and not very pretty. Little caterpillar, are you crying? Oh! Little caterpillar, do you know that God has beautiful clothes planned for you?**

ASK
• Boys and girls, what would you say to comfort the caterpillar?

SAY Our Bible story says that those who cry will laugh someday. When you said those kind things to the caterpillar, you were seeing some things God's way. You see, caterpillars don't know that one day they'll be beautiful butterflies. But as they follow God's plan, that's exactly what happens.

The world might see this little guy and say he's not worth very much. He doesn't have big strong muscles or pretty hair, and he can't write his name or prove how smart he is. But you can look at him from God's point of view—you know what God has planned. It won't happen today, will it? But, if the caterpillar is patient and keeps following God's path, he will be all God created him to be.

Sometimes kids don't know all the things God has planned for them, either. But, as kids look for and follow God's kingdom, wonderful things happen.

Would you like to make caterpillar puppets of your own to remind you to look at things the way God sees them?

Help the children apply the glue and eyes. It may be easier to apply the tape to their fingernails, then press on the pompoms.

SAY Remember that God sees things differently than we do, and he is honored when we seek the ways of his kingdom.

(continued from page 124)

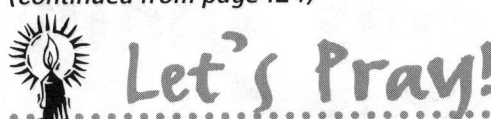
Let's Pray!

The Offering

SAY Think of some things that you really love having or being. Perhaps you might say your video games. Or you might really love being the best one in your class at reading or math. God wants us to put our relationship with him above those things.

ASK • Are you willing to seek God more than the things you love?

SAY As you place your offering in the bowl, tell God that you want to seek him more than the things in this world. Let's sing "We Want to See Jesus Lifted High" while we give our offering.

 **track 19**   Sing "We Want to See Jesus Lifted High."
Lyrics and motions are in the back of this book.

I Just Seek You

SAY We've seen lots of illusions and tricks this morning. The world is full of untruths and half-truths—some of them quite believable. We can get very confused by what the world wants us to believe. But God is honored when we seek his kingdom. It's not enough for us to try to understand what's going on. We need Jesus' wisdom. If you want to seek God's kingdom, pray the words "I just seek you" when I pause in this prayer we'll pray together.

PRAY Lord, I don't always understand what's right, so...[I just seek you].
The world can be a pretty confusing place, so...[I just seek you].
Help me to honor you as...[I just seek you].
In Jesus' name, amen.

Quiet Reflection

If possible, dim the lights and light a candle for this activity.

SAY Sometimes we need to get away from distractions and seek God quietly. When we quiet our minds and seek God, he guides us with his light and love.

Find a quiet spot in the room, and spend a few minutes putting away distractions and asking God to tell you how you can honor him by seeking his kingdom today.

 **track 6**   Play "Praise, I Will Praise You, Lord."

Allow the children to pray quietly for a few minutes before ending the session in prayer.

PRAY God, help us remember to put away the distractions and illusions of the world and seek you this week. Guide us and direct us as we seek your kingdom. In Jesus' name, amen.

Jesus Teaches About Loving Enemies

Luke 6:27-38

Worship Theme: We worship God by loving others.

A Look at the Session

Session Sequence	What Children Will Do	Supplies
Getting Started	Find a warm welcome at children's church.	**KidsOwn Worship Kit:** Songs From FaithWeaver, Vol. 6 **Classroom Supplies:** CD player
Let's Praise God! 1 (up to 25 minutes)	**Sing:** • "My God Is" (track 4) • "Jesus Loves Me Rock" (track 7) • "His Love" (track 12) • "Your Everlasting Love" (track 17) • "I Want to Be Like Jesus" (track 15)	**KidsOwn Worship Kit:** Songs From FaithWeaver, Vol. 6; Lyrics Transparencies **Classroom Supplies:** CD player, overhead projector, cups, unsweetened cocoa powder, milk, thermal container, sugar, spoons

2 Let's Learn the Point! — PRESCHOOL ACTIVITIES (up to 25 minutes)

What Children Will Do	Supplies
Happy and Sad—Help tell about the golden rule.	**Classroom Supplies:** Poster board, markers
✳ Doing Good to Others—Play a game to learn about loving others.	**Classroom Supplies:** Heart stickers, masking tape, treats
Right Hand, Left Hand—Learn a finger play about God's way.	

2 Let's Learn the Point! — ELEMENTARY ACTIVITIES (up to 25 minutes)

What Children Will Do	Supplies
✳ Keep Away—Play a game to explore Jesus' teachings.	**Classroom Supplies:** Newspaper
✳ And Now, Here's What We Think—Watch a video that explores what the world would be like if everyone followed Jesus' teachings.	**KidsOwn Worship Kit:** KidsOwn Worship Video: "And Now, Here's What We Think" **Classroom Supplies:** TV, VCR
Job Descriptions—Personalize Luke 6:27-31, 35-36.	**Classroom Supplies:** Bibles, paper, pencils

Session Sequence	What Children Will Do	Supplies
Let's Pray! 3 (up to 10 minutes)	**The Offering**—Offer their gifts to God and remember to do to others as they would have others do to them.	**Classroom Supplies:** Offering bowls, slips of paper, pens
	Love With the Love of Jesus—Think about what it means to love with the love of Jesus as they sing.	**KidsOwn Worship Kit:** Songs From FaithWeaver, Vol. 6: "Love With the Love of Jesus" (track 16) **Classroom Supplies:** CD player
	Do to Others—Participate in a responsive prayer to show their love of God through their actions.	

✳ Starred activities can be used successfully with preschool and elementary children together.

Customize your session to fit your needs. You can separate preschoolers and elementary children for Section 2.

Or, if you keep the children all together for the entire worship session, we suggest you choose from the starred activities.

Why We Worship

We worship a God who is merciful: He's kind to the ungrateful and wicked. Worldly standards of good behavior are based on an eye-for-an-eye concept of fairness. Jesus' gives us another standard of conduct, one that's in sharp contrast to the "Don't-get-mad—get-even!" world we live in. According to Jesus, we have the responsibility to "get over it," not for the sake of the wrong-doer, but for the sake of God.

When we overcome our natural tendency to demand earthly fairness, we honor God. God asks us to love our enemies, to do good to those who hate us, to pray for those who mistreat us. Doing so moves our focus from ourselves and our rights to God and his mercy. When we focus on God's kindness, we have the power to love others around us—even the difficult ones.

Bible Background

Luke 6:27-38

Luke 6:27-38 is a continuation of Jesus' Sermon on the Plain. In it Jesus teaches what it really means to love. The Jews knew what enemies were, and when Jesus talked about people who cursed them, mistreated them, struck them, and stole from them, the Jews likely thought of the Romans. It would have been tough for Jews to accept the idea that they should love their oppressors.

But Jesus wasn't saying that they should have warm feelings toward their enemies. Instead, Jesus was telling them to love their enemies as a conscious act of will, to act in ways that would please their enemies, to behave toward them as a merciful God would. Jesus' command runs exactly counter to the human impulse. Even so, this is the law of love that God wants to see in the hearts of those who follow Jesus.

Jesus also points out the emptiness of loving only those who love us. That's easy! Our love shouldn't be based on the expectation of being loved in return; instead we should look forward to a heavenly reward because we have treated people as God wants us to treat them (Luke 6:35).

In his summary of this teaching (Luke 6:35-36), Jesus stresses the importance of the principle he has explained. Our very position as children of God is at stake. If we are "sons of the Most High," we will live and love in the way Jesus describes. When people watch us, they should see our merciful God in our attitudes and actions.

Skits and Puppets

In the KidsOwn Worship Kit, you'll find a collection of skits titled, "KidsOwn Worship Skits." The skits are designed to be used with Theophilus the FaithRetriever puppet during the preschool activities. You can purchase a Theo puppet at your local Christian bookstore.

Song Lyrics and Motions

To make the worship session go more smoothly, tear out the lyrics sheets at the back of this book and keep them in a separate folder. Each week, pull out only the sheets you need for the day's worship session.

Before Worship

Before the worship session, prepare hot cocoa using *unsweetened* cocoa powder and omitting any sugar mentioned in the preparation instructions. Put the cocoa in a thermal container.

 Set up a TV and VCR, and cue the *KidsOwn Worship Video* to the "And Now, Here's What We Think" segment. Watch the segment at least once before the worship session so you'll be familiar with it.

Arrival Time

Play *Songs From FaithWeaver, Vol. 6* as children arrive. Greet children by name, and say, "I'm so glad you're here today! Find a friend, and ask your friend what the golden rule is."

Leader SkillBuilder

Not all the children will understand the idea of doing to others as you would have them do to you. Many will already evaluate behavior the world's way and may even need to look out for themselves because of a less than optimal home situation. Be patient when teaching a concept that goes so much against the flow of society.

When all the children have arrived, gather them around you.

SAY Welcome! As I greeted each of you, I asked you to find a friend and ask that friend what the golden rule is.

ASK • What answers did you get?

SAY I've heard some pretty strange explanations in the past. Some people think it means the person with the most gold makes the rules! But the golden rule really has nothing to do with wealth or the color gold. *Golden* is an old way of saying "most important."

Luke 6:31 says, "Do to others as you would have them do to you," and verses 27-38 tell us how to do this. The golden rule is God's idea. Let's remember who God is and why we can trust his ideas for us. The next song will help us remember who he is.

 Sing "My God Is."
Lyrics and motions are in the back of this book.

SAY As our creator, God has some pretty good ideas about how we should live life, doesn't he? Jesus is God. And Jesus is the one who first told us about the golden rule. It's a great plan for getting along with others, but it's much more than that! It's a way of communicating his love to others. Let's sing about who he is and how much he loves us.

 Sing "Jesus Loves Me Rock."
Lyrics and motions are in the back of this book.

SAY I've prepared a treat for you today. It's hot cocoa made from scratch. Since it's special, I'm going to serve it to you, then walk you through a couple of steps to help you appreciate it. Don't taste it until everyone is served so we can appreciate the cocoa together. Serve all the kids a cup of hot cocoa and a spoon. The more cocoa you pour into a cup, the more sugar kids will need to add, so keep the quantities small.

SAY Stir the cup a little so you can get a good whiff of how rich and chocolaty this cocoa is. Mmm. Now taste just a little.

ASK • What do you think?
   • What did my words—what I told you—lead you to believe?

SAY I built up the benefits of this cocoa, but it isn't as great as I made it sound, is it? The cocoa I gave you is bitter.

ASK • If I *tell* you how wonderful my God is then *show* you some nasty or bitter attitudes instead of God's sweetness, what might you think of God and Christians?
   • If I *tell* you my God is love, but I don't *show* love to others, what might you think of God and Christians?

SAY I'm going to let each of you add sugar to your cocoa so you can really enjoy it. As you enjoy the cocoa, think about sharing God's love. If we want to share God's love with others, we need to give them the whole "recipe"— we can't leave out any of the parts. God's love is sweet. It is kind and merciful. Let's worship God as we think about his love.

 track 12
Sing "His Love."
Lyrics and motions are in the back of this book.

Worship Leader Tip

This activity works best if you can offer your kids sugar packets rather than passing a sugar bowl around.

SAY That's a wonderful kind of love—higher than the highest mountains, deeper than the deepest seas, stretching to the farthest horizon. But there is one more thing about Jesus' love. It never ends. Never. It is everlasting, no matter what mistakes we make. Let's praise Jesus as we sing this song about his wonderful, everlasting love.

 track 17
Sing "Your Everlasting Love."
Lyrics and motions are in the back of this book.

SAY God is always loving—that's what we mean when we say God has "everlasting love." But *we* aren't always loving.

ASK • When is it hardest for you to be loving and kind?

SAY When God's love reaches to you and touches your heart, you can be like Jesus by loving others. You can treat others the way you want to be treated, even if they are unkind to you. Let's sing this song as a prayer to the Lord, asking him to help us be like him and treat others the way he wants us to treat them.

 track 15
Sing "I Want to Be Like Jesus."
Lyrics and motions are in the back of this book.

PRAY God, sometimes it's hard to show your love to people who are mean or ungrateful. But we know you can help us. And we are willing to try to love others because we love you and want to honor you. In Jesus' name, amen.

Let's Learn the Point!

PRESCHOOL ACTIVITIES, pp. 133–134

At this time, have the preschool helper invite the preschoolers to go to their own room for this section of activities. Tear out the Preschool Activities page, and give it to the preschool leader. Have the preschool leader bring the preschoolers back to participate in the prayer time with the older children. If you prefer to keep all the children together, do the starred activities. They will work well with both elementary and preschool children.

ELEMENTARY ACTIVITIES

* Keep Away

Have children form groups of three. Give each group one sheet of newspaper, and have them crumple it to form a ball. Have the children sit on the floor in their groups so that one person is sitting between the other two to play a game of Keep Away. Give each child three pieces of candy.

SAY Each group has its own ball. I've also given each group member three pieces of candy. You can do whatever you want with the candy as you play, except put it in your mouth. You can give it to someone else, or you can keep it. You'll play Keep Away, but you must remain seated at all times.

Let the kids start tossing the paper ball and trying to keep it away from the person in the middle. As soon as the middle person gets the ball, he or she will trade places with one of the throwers. After two minutes of play, if the middle people have not yet traded places, have them do so. Make sure that each child gets a chance to be in the middle.

ASK • What did you think of this game?
• When you were in the middle, what strategy did you use to get the paper ball?
• Did any of you use the candy to bribe your group members to give you the paper ball? Raise your hand if someone used candy to try to bribe another player and get out of the middle.

SAY Raise your hand if someone in your group kept the candy for him or herself.

Raise your hand if someone in your group gave candy to someone just because that person asked for a piece.

Raise your hand if someone in the group gave a piece of candy to one of the tossers after he or she was out of the middle.

ASK • Which action with the candy is most like this passage of Scripture: "But I tell you who hear me: Love your enemies, do good to those who hate you. Bless those who curse you, pray for those who mistreat you"?
• Which action is most like this Scripture: "Give to everyone who asks you, and if anyone takes what belongs to you, do not demand it back"?
• Why would anyone want to give candy to someone who was being mean, even if it's just in a game?
• Why would anyone want to give his or her last candy (or first) to someone just because the person asked?

(continued on page 135)

Preschool Activities

12

Jesus Teaches About Loving Enemies Luke 6:27-38

Worship Theme: We worship God by loving others.

Using Theo

Consider using Theophilus the FaithRetriever puppet today in these ways.

- Have Theo lead the preschoolers from the main worship area to the preschool room.

- Have Theo point to the large happy face or sad face in the "Happy and Sad" activity.

- See the KidsOwn Worship Kit for a puppet skit written for today's worship session.

Happy and Sad

Before this activity, prepare a large happy face and a large sad face on pieces of poster board.

SAY I'm going to tell you what Jesus said when he taught a very large group of people. I need your help, though. I'll be talking about doing good and about people who aren't nice. Every time I talk about something not nice, I'll point to the sad face, and I want you to say "Boo!" When I talk about something good, I'll point to the happy face, and you can say, "Yeah!" Let's practice before I begin telling you what Jesus taught this big group of people. Point to the sad face and help the children respond with a loud "Boo!" Then point to the happy face, and encourage the children to respond with "Yeah!"

Jesus wanted people to know how to treat each other, so he told them how. Jesus knows there are people who will be your enemies. Point to the sad face. **But Jesus said to love them.** Point to the happy face. **He knows there might be people who hate you.** Point to the sad face. **But Jesus said to do good to them.** Point to the happy face. **There will probably be people who say bad things to you and do mean things to you.** Point to the sad face. **But Jesus said to pray for them and bless them.** Point to the happy face. **Jesus said he wants us to be nice to all people and treat them the way we would like to be treated. This is called the golden rule.** Point to the happy face again.

Jesus wants people who follow him to act differently than people who don't know him. He wants us to follow this rule too!

✻ Doing Good to Others

Use masking tape to mark a square on the floor. The square should be big enough to allow all the children to move freely in it. Give each preschooler two heart stickers.

SAY Our Bible story today tells us that if someone asks us for something, we should give it without expecting to get it back. In fact, Jesus told people that, if someone asks for your coat, you should give even more than the person asked for.

Each of you has two stickers. You're going to walk around the square and shake hands with your friends. If someone asks you for a sticker, you can give the person one sticker or two

(continued on page 134)

(continued from page 133)

stickers. But as soon as you have no stickers left, you have to stand outside the square.

Walk through the game with a couple of children until the kids understand how to play. Then let the children play the game. Join in the game yourself, and ask the children to give you a sticker. If you have any helpers, have them play the game too.

Lead the first child who gives away both stickers to the edge of the square, and give him or her the treat you've prepared. Soon the children will be trying to give their stickers away rather than trying to keep them. Continue playing until all the children have received treats.

ASK • **When you didn't know you were going to get something good at the end of the game, how did you feel about giving away your stickers?**

SAY You know, pleasing God is the best treat of all! We worship God as we do what he wants us to do. God wants us to do nice things to show our love for others even when it's hard. You were all very good at giving your stickers away. I'm going to thank you for that by giving the stickers back to you now! Give the children two stickers each.

Right Hand, Left Hand

Teach this finger play to your preschoolers to help them remember Jesus' teachings.

This is my right hand.	*(Hold out your right hand, palm up.)*
I use it to do good.	*(Wave your right hand, palm up, back and forth.)*
This is my left hand.	*(Hold out your left hand, palm up, next to your right hand.)*
I treat others as I should.	*(Clap your hands together.)*
Right hand,	*(Hold your right hand out, palm up.)*
Left hand,	*(Hold your left hand out, palm up.)*
Love every day.	*(Clap your hands together.)*
Right hand,	*(Hold right hand out, palm up.)*
Left hand,	*(Hold left hand out, palm up.)*
This is Jesus' way.	*(Point up with one finger.)*

(continued from page 132)

SAY God asks us to do just those kinds of things. He asks us to give to people who might be ungrateful and to loan without expecting our things to be returned. There's only one reason to live that way. Not because we think there's something really great about losing, but because being *willing* to lose in order to love people pleases God. We worship God by loving others in the way he asks us to.

✽ And Now, Here's What We Think

 Show the video segment titled "And Now, Here's What We Think." The segment shows how several children think the world might look like if people loved their enemies.

ASK • Do you agree with these kids about what the world would be like if people loved their enemies? Explain.
• What do you think the world would look like?
• Do you think the world will ever really be like this? Why or why not?
• Why do you think Jesus wants us to love our enemies?
• Who can you show love to—even though that person might have been mean to you?

SAY Loving our enemies can be really hard. But it's what God wants us to do. Loving others honors God.

Job Description

Have children form groups of three.

SAY Many people who work in large businesses have what are called job descriptions. A job description describes what an employee is expected to do as part of his or her job. In some ways, the Scripture passage we looked at today is like a job description. It's a list of things that people who want to honor God are expected to do.

In your group, choose a Reader, a Recorder, and a Reporter. The Reader will read the Scripture, the Recorder will record your group's thoughts, and the Reporter will share the thoughts with the whole group. Allow the children time to follow your instructions.

Here's your task. Look at Luke 6:27-31 and 35-36. For each action Jesus tells people to do, tell something similar he might say to someone in your school. For example, if the Bible words say "If someone takes your cloak, do not stop him from taking your tunic," you might say, "If someone wants your pencil, let him have your eraser, too."

Give each group a pencil, a piece of paper, and a Bible. Allow groups to complete the job descriptions, then ask them to share their ideas with the rest of the children. If you have extra time, you might ask the children to tell which of all the job description items they heard would be hardest for them to do.

 Let's Pray!

The Offering

Hand each child a slip of paper and something to write with.

SAY Today as we take our offering, I want you to write the name of one person who has not been kind to you on your piece of paper. As the offering bowl comes by you, put the piece of paper in it, and ask God to help you love that person and treat him or her in a way that would honor God. Remember—as you show God's love to that person, you are worshipping God in your everyday life. If you can't think of a name to put on your paper, write the name of a friend who might need God's help in a hard situation. If you have an offering today, put that in the bowl also.

Choose several children to help collect the offering. Encourage older children to assist younger children with the writing if necessary.

Love With the Love of Jesus

SAY Treating others with love and kindness can be very hard to do. Only Jesus' love for us can make us able to love others his way. Think about what it means to love as Jesus does as you worship him with this song.

 Sing "Love With the Love of Jesus."
Lyrics and motions are in the back of this book.

Do to Others

Ask children to form two groups. Explain that the children in Group 1 will say, **"Do to others..."** when you point to them and the children in Group 2 will say, **"...as you would have them do to you,"** when you point to them.

SAY Let's pray together to God today. I'll start. Then I'll point to Group 1, and you'll say "Do to others..." Then I'll point to Group 2, and you'll say, "...as you would have them do to you."

PRAY Dear God, when others are my enemies, help me to remember to... Point to the two groups in turn.

When others say bad things and do mean things to me, help me to remember to... Point to the two groups in turn.

When people don't give things back, and treat me badly, help me to remember to... Point to the two groups in turn.

In Jesus' name, amen.

SAY Every day this week, remember that you are worshipping God as you allow Jesus to help you treat others as you would like to be treated.

Jesus Teaches About Good Fruit

Luke 6:43-44

Worship Theme: God helps us grow.

A Look at the Session

Session Sequence	What Children Will Do	Supplies
⏱ **Getting Started**	Find a warm welcome at children's church.	**KidsOwn Worship Kit:** *Songs From FaithWeaver, Vol. 6* **Classroom Supplies:** CD player, growth chart
1 Let's Praise God! (up to 25 minutes)	**Sing:** • "We Want to See Jesus Lifted High" (track 19) • "Love With the Love of Jesus" (track 16) • "Praise, I Will Praise You, Lord" (track 6) • "I Love You, Lord" (track 18) • "Seek Ye First" (track 13)	**KidsOwn Worship Kit:** *Songs From FaithWeaver, Vol. 6;* Lyrics Transparencies **Classroom Supplies:** CD player, overhead projector, step stool, to-do list, chalkboard, chalk

2 Let's Learn the Point! — PRESCHOOL ACTIVITIES (up to 25 minutes)

What Children Will Do	Supplies
The Right Fruit—Learn how God helps people grow to produce good fruit.	**Classroom Supplies:** Scissors, masking tape, copies of "The Right Fruit" handout (p. 146)
✳ **Bearing Fruit**—Paint fruit vines to remember the good fruit God wants them to grow.	**Classroom Supplies:** Paint smocks, butcher paper, washable tempera paint, water, paintbrush, sponges, straws, marker, wet wipes
God Is Helping Me Grow—Praise God for helping them grow in many ways.	

2 Let's Learn the Point! — ELEMENTARY ACTIVITIES (up to 25 minutes)

What Children Will Do	Supplies
✳ **Growing Flowers**—Explore how it's necessary to receive God's help personally in order to grow.	**KidsOwn Worship Kit:** Magic Flower **Classroom Supplies:** Tray, water, plastic wrap
✳ **Orchards**—Watch and discuss the video segment.	**KidsOwn Worship Kit:** *KidsOwn Worship Video:* "Orchards" **Classroom Supplies:** VCR, TV
Fruit of the Spirit—Design trees that define the fruit of the Spirit.	**Classroom Supplies:** Butcher paper, dictionaries, markers

Session Sequence	What Children Will Do	Supplies
✋ **3 Let's Pray!** (up to 10 minutes)	**The Offering**—Measure the height of their growing offering.	**Classroom Supplies:** Glass jar, ruler, transparent tape
	Growing Fruit—Thank God for growing good fruit in their lives.	**KidsOwn Worship Kit:** Magic Flower **Classroom Supplies:** "Fruit of the Spirit" trees
	I Want to Be Like Jesus—Sing a song as a prayer.	**KidsOwn Worship Kit:** *Songs From FaithWeaver, Vol. 6:* "I Want to Be Like Jesus" (track 15) **Classroom Supplies:** CD player

✳ Starred activities can be used successfully with preschool and elementary children together.

Customize your session to fit your needs. You can separate preschoolers and elementary children for Section 2.

Or, if you keep the children all together for the entire worship session, we suggest you choose from the starred activities.

Why We Worship

The Bible tells us that God intends for his people to grow in faith, in character, and in good works. The Bible promises that "the righteous will flourish like a palm tree, they will grow like a cedar of Lebanon" (Psalm 92:12). John 15 tells us that, if we abide in Christ and if Christ abides in us, we will grow into the people God wants us to be. God helps us grow. What a mighty God we serve!

Skits and Puppets

In the KidsOwn Worship Kit, you'll find a collection of skits titled, "KidsOwn Worship Skits." The skits are designed to be used with Theophilus the FaithRetriever puppet during the preschool activities. You can purchase a Theo puppet at your local Christian bookstore.

Bible Background

Luke 6:43-45

In his references to good and bad trees in this passage, Jesus is obviously drawing an analogy to the fruit that people bear. Notice that the distinction is not between healthy apple trees and diseased apple trees. It is between fruit trees and thorns or briers; it is the kind of tree that makes the difference. Many kinds of trees look good but don't produce fruit. So it is with people. Jesus seems to be saying that a person who is not really a servant of God, no matter how good he or she seems to be, cannot possibly produce fruit for him. Conversely, someone who really is God's servant will automatically produce fruit.

In Luke 6:45, Jesus expounds on the principle he introduced in the tree metaphor. What comes out of us through our speech and behavior flows from what is within. If what is inside us is good and God-honoring, our lives will honor God. If what is inside us is evil, our lives will not honor God. No matter how hard we try to make good impressions, no one will be fooled for long if our hearts are deceitful.

# Getting Started

Before Worship

Before the worship session, attach a growth chart or measuring tape to the entrance children will use. Make an average day's to-do list for Let's Praise God!

 Set up a TV and VCR. Cue the *KidsOwn Worship Video* to the "Orchards" segment. You'll want to watch the segment at least once before the children arrive.

Put the Magic Flower on a tray, and cover it with plastic wrap.

Tape a ruler to the side of a glass jar to use during Let's Pray!

Arrival Time

Play *Songs From FaithWeaver, Vol. 6* as children arrive. Greet children by name, and measure each one.

SAY **You're growing on the outside just as God planned. He helps you grow on the inside, too.**

# Let's Praise God!

Have the children stand.

SAY **Welcome to children's church! Let's lift Jesus high! When we praise Jesus—when we tell others how wonderful he is—we lift him high. We show the world that Jesus is more important and more wonderful than anyone or anything else!**

Stand on the step stool.

SAY **Jesus is Lord of my life. I lift him high right now.**

Invite the children to take turns standing on the step stool and praising Jesus to lift him high. Stand next to the step stool to help children step on and off safely.

SAY **Now let's lift him high in song. Let's sing "We Want to See Jesus Lifted High."**

 Sing "We Want to See Jesus Lifted High."
Lyrics and motions are in the back of this book.

SAY **Another way to lift Jesus high is to love other people the way Jesus would love them. When we show Jesus' love to others, they see how much Jesus cares for them, and they learn to love him too. Jesus' love is special. It is deeper than any other kind of love. Let's ask God to help us love others with Jesus' love. Let's sing "Love With the Love of Jesus."**

 Sing "Love With the Love of Jesus."
Lyrics and motions are in the back of this book.

SAY **Listen while I tell you a story from the Bible.**

Song Lyrics and Motions

To make the worship session go more smoothly, tear out the lyrics sheets at the back of this book and keep them in a separate folder. Each week, pull out only the sheets you need for the day's worship session.

Leader SkillBuilder

Managing a large class requires keeping control at all times. To keep chaos from taking over in activities like the first one in Let's Praise God!, run the activity like a graduation ceremony. Have the children stand one row at a time. Have them exit to the right, move to the front of the class to praise Jesus, then enter their rows from the left. As one row finishes, have the next stand. Continue until every child has had a turn.

If children sit on the floor rather than in chairs, have children form a large circle around the room. Have them walk in a circle to the right, stopping to give each child a turn to speak as he or she reaches the front. The formality will encourage more children to participate. It will also give the children a sense of importance as they take part in a classroom *event*.

SAY There was once a beautiful vine. It produced sweet, wonderful fruit. A wise gardener tended the vine. He cared for it lovingly. Some of the branches of the vine were dry and withered. They didn't produce any fruit at all. The gardener knew that those dry, withered branches were not good for the vine because they pulled energy away from the healthy branches. So the wise gardener cut off the dry, withered branches.

The wise gardener didn't stop there. He knew that even the healthy branches of the vine could be better. The gardener trimmed them and cleaned them so they would bear even more fruit.

The Bible tells us that Jesus is the vine and God is the gardener that tends the vine. We're like the branches—we're connected to Jesus—and the fruit we grow is goodness and patience and kindness. God helps us grow to be like Jesus so that we can love others with Jesus' love. He helps us grow the way a gardener helps the branches of a vine to grow. The Bible says that Jesus is the vine, God is the gardener, and we are the branches.

ASK • How does a gardener help the branches of a vine to grow?

SAY The gardener waters the vine, makes sure it has plenty of sunlight, keeps bugs away, and prunes it. That means he cuts off the dead branches so healthy branches can grow.

The vine helps the branches grow by sending water and food to each one. Jesus gives us everything we need to grow healthy and strong, so we can show his love to others.

God helps us grow. As we grow to be the people he wants us to be, showing Jesus' love to others, we bring glory and honor to God. Just as a vine is the source of water and food for its branches, Jesus is the source of our joy as he helps us grow! Let's glorify his name right now by singing "Praise, I Will Praise You, Lord." Everyone stand up and sing.

 Sing "Praise, I Will Praise You, Lord."
Lyrics and motions are in the back of this book.

SAY God helps us grow. God fills us with love for others. God gives us everything we need to be the people he wants us to be. I love him! Don't you? Let's sing "I Love You, Lord."

 Sing "I Love You, Lord."
Lyrics and motions are in the back of this book.

Let the children sit down. Show them your to-do list.

SAY Sometimes, when I have a lot to do, I make a list. I call this my to-do list because it is a list of things to do. Here is my list. Read the list aloud.

Some days, I have so much to do that I know I won't get it all done! On those days, I have to choose the most important things to do. Let's make a to-do list of our own and decide what activities are most important.

Have children call out things they might do on an average day. Write their responses on the chalkboard or on newsprint. Then help the children number all answers in order of importance.

SAY It can be hard to choose wisely, but homework is more important than television. Going to school is more important than going to a friend's house.

It's nice when we have time to do everything we want to do, but when we don't have time, we have to choose wisely.

SAY Keeping our priorities straight helps us grow. Jesus gives everything we need to grow, and he helps our branch of the vine grow more fruit to glorify God's name and bring other people to Jesus. We need to let Jesus work in our lives. Let's sing "Seek Ye First" to remind us of the right order of priorities.

 Sing "Seek Ye First."
Lyrics and motions are in the back of this book.

PRAY God, we love you. We want to glorify you. You deserve all honor and praise. Thank you for helping us grow so we can show others Jesus' love and bring more people to you. We want to grow good fruit for your kingdom because we love you, Lord! In Jesus' name, amen.

Let's Learn the Point!

PRESCHOOL ACTIVITIES, pp. 143–144

At this time, have the preschool helper invite the preschoolers to go to their own room for this section of activities. Tear out the Preschool Activities page, and give it to the preschool leader. Have the preschool leader bring the preschoolers back to participate in the prayer time with the older children. If you prefer to keep all the children together, do the starred activities. They will work well with both elementary and preschool children.

ELEMENTARY ACTIVITIES

✳ Growing Flowers

Show the children the Magic Flower from the KidsOwn Worship Kit.

ASK • What do flowers need to grow?

SAY Let's give this flower some water. Ask a child to pour the packet of liquid into the tray. Have everyone watch the flower for thirty seconds.

ASK • The directions say to add this liquid. Why do you think the flower isn't growing?

SAY Let's set the flower aside for awhile. Then we'll come back to it to see if there have been any changes.

Set the flower aside while you do the next activity. There will be a discussion about the flower at the end of the next activity.

✳ Orchards

 Watch the video segment titled "Orchards."

ASK • What was this video about?
• What did you find interesting or surprising about this video?
• How does knowing that God is helping you grow the way a farmer takes care of the orchard make you feel?

> **Worship Leader Tip**
>
> The manufacturer has trademarked this product "Magic Flower." If you prefer not to use the word "magic," feel free to substitute another word, such as "crystal" or "amazing." Remove the packaging, and put it where the children can't see it.

Bring out the Magic Flower from the previous activity. The flower should just be starting to show the growth of crystals at the ends of the "branches."

ASK • Do you notice anything different about the flower now?
• Why do you think it took awhile for the flower to start growing?
• How is the way the flower grows like the way a Christian grows? Why?
• The flower needed water to grow. What do Christians need to help them grow?
• In what ways is God helping you grow?

SAY God helps us grow in all kinds of ways. And just like this flower, we grow little by little every day. Sometimes we don't even notice our growth because it happens so slowly. But God promises us that he will help us grow until we're exactly what he wants us to be.

Set the flower aside again to bring out during the prayer time.

Fruit of the Spirit

SAY The Bible tells us that Christians grow just like flowers or fruit in a garden. These are the things that grow in us: Galatians 5:22-23 says, "But the fruit of the Spirit is love, joy, peace, patience, kindness, goodness, faithfulness, gentleness and self-control. Against such things there is no law." God's Spirit in our lives grows all these good things. Let's learn more about the fruit of the Spirit.

Divide the class into nine groups—it's OK if only one child is in each group. Give each group a square of butcher paper, and provide several dictionaries.

Assign one fruit of the Spirit—love, joy, peace, patience, kindness, goodness, faithfulness, gentleness, and self-control—to each group. If you have fewer than nine children, have the children take more than one fruit each. Have each group look up the definition of its word. Then have the children design trees for their fruit. The designs should include the group's word and its definition. Encourage kids to use their imaginations as they design trees that characterize the fruits of God's Spirit. Display the trees around the room.

Have the children sit near their trees. Ask each group to tell an act that might grow from its tree, and one that could never grow on their tree.

SAY Just as plums only grow on plum trees and apples only grow on apple trees, the trees you designed can only bear fruit of their own kind.

ASK • What does that tell you about your actions if God is growing the fruits of the Spirit in you?

SAY God helps us grow in these characteristics just as surely as he helps our physical bodies grow. When we are nourished by him, kindness, love, gentleness, peace, and all the other "fruits" are the things we can show to others. Those things honor and glorify God, our gardener.

 Let's Pray!

The Offering

Place the glass jar with the ruler attached on a table at the front of the room.

(continued on page 145)

Preschool Activities

Jesus Teaches About Good Fruit Luke 6:43-44

Worship Theme: God helps us grow.

Using Theo

Consider using Theophilus the FaithRetriever puppet today in these ways:

• Have Theo lead the preschoolers from the main worship area to the preschool room.

• Have Theo lead the song "God Is Helping Me Grow."

• See the KidsOwn Worship Kit for a puppet skit written for today's worship session.

The Right Fruit

Before class, make one copy of "The Right Fruit" handout (p. 146) for each child. Use scissors or a paper cutter to separate the four sections.

SAY One day, Jesus told a story about trees. He told this story to help us understand how God helps us grow. Jesus said that each tree grows its own kind of fruit.

Have the children stand and pretend to be trees.

SAY You are all apple trees. You can only grow apples.

Have the children pretend to be pear trees.

ASK • What kind of fruit does a pear tree grow?

Continue, having the children pretend to be different kinds of trees. Ask what kind of fruit each tree grows. Then have the children sit down.

SAY Jesus said people grow like trees. If there is good in their hearts, they do good things. If there is bad in their hearts, they do bad things. But God helps us grow to do good things. When we let him take care of our hearts, he makes our hearts good, so we can do good things for him. The good we do is called our fruit. Let's be good fruit trees.

Have the children stand and pretend to be trees again. Use masking tape loops to hang the fruit from the handout on the children's "tree-branch" arms.

ASK • What kind of fruit are you growing?

Help the children understand what is happening in each handout picture.

SAY Showing love to others, helping our parents, sharing with friends, and talking to God are good things to do. These things are good fruit! Let's ask God to help us grow good fruit.

PRAY Lord, we want to grow good fruit. Thank you for your help. Help us grow to do the good things you want us to do. We want to grow good because we love you. In Jesus' name, amen.

✱ Bearing Fruit

Before class, dampen one or more sponges, and put a different fruit-colored washable tempera on each sponge. If you'd like, you can add a bit of fruit-scented extract to the paint. You'll also need green washable tempera paint thinned with water to the consistency of light cream.

(continued on page 144)

(continued from page 143)

Have the children sit around tables covered with butcher paper. Give each a paint smock (old shirts worn backward work well as smocks) and a straw.

SAY God helps us grow. He gives us everything we need to grow the way he wants us to. He helps us to be the loving people he wants us to be. We're going to do a project to show everyone that we know God helps us to grow and bear good fruit to honor him.

Use a paintbrush to put drops of green paint around the edges of the paper. Show the children how to blow on the paint through their straws to make the paint drops *grow* into long thin lines. If necessary, add paint drops along the children's lines so they can make the lines longer.

ASK • How did you make the paint lines grow?

SAY You gave the paint what it needed by blowing air in a certain direction.

ASK • What does God give us to help us grow?

SAY Let's help these green vines have fruit! Raise your hand to tell me one good thing God can help you do or grow to do. When you tell me something, you can press your thumb on one of the sponges and make thumbprint fruit on a vine.

> ### Preschool Leader Tip
>
> Watch the children carefully to keep them from getting carried away during this activity. They could be tempted to blow paint onto the table or toward each other. If possible, invite extra helpers in for this project. If extra help is not possible, let one or two children work at a time while the others watch. Limit time with the paint and straws so children will be less likely to exercise their creativity in messy ways.

For Extra Impact

Give the children fruit snacks as they finish, and have them be seated in a designated area until the other children finish.

As each child finishes making thumbprints, wipe his or her hands with a wet wipe. Let the children write their names somewhere on the paper. Print "God Helps Us Grow" on the butcher paper, and display the banner in a prominent place.

God Is Helping Me Grow

Have the children sit in a circle.

SAY God helps you grow. God helps you grow taller. God helps you learn new things. God helps you develop strong muscles. God helps you do good things for other people. God helps you learn to know and love him! God is good! Let's thank him.

Teach God Is Helping Me Grow to the tune of "I'm a Little Tea Pot."

> **God is helping me grow big and strong.**
> **I learn new things all the year long.**
> **I thank God for helping me grow**
> **To do the things that please him so.**

At the end of the song, ask a child to name something he or she has recently learned. Have the class say, "Thank you, God, for helping us grow!" Sing the song several times, making sure each child gets a chance to share.

(continued from page 142)

SAY God helps us grow. Let's thank him by giving offerings that will help his kingdom grow. As you give your offerings, we'll measure their growth on the ruler.

PRAY Thank you, God, for helping us grow. We want to be more like you. Use our offerings now to help others grow and to build your kingdom as only you can do. In Jesus' name, amen.

Let the children put their offerings in the jar. For fun, tell the children how tall their offering is. You may wish to continue this activity for several weeks as you reinforce the point that God helps us grow.

Growing Fruit

Point to the "Fruit of the Spirit" trees, made earlier.

SAY God helps us grow on the outside and on the inside. Inside, he grows spiritual fruit—love, joy, peace, patience, kindness, goodness, gentleness, faithfulness, and self-control.

ASK • Which fruit do you think God most wants to grow in your life now?

Have children stand by the picture that shows their answer.

Show the children the Magic Flower and point out how much it has grown during the worship session.

SAY We can count on God to help us grow little by little every day. Let's thank God for growing good fruit in our lives. And let's thank God for being faithful in helping us grow every day.

Let volunteers say sentence prayers, thanking God for helping them grow.

I Want to Be Like Jesus

SAY I want to be like Jesus. Don't you? While on earth, Jesus lived the way God wants all people to live. He's a perfect example of what God wants us to be! As God helps us grow, he makes us more like Jesus. He gives us hearts that are pure and true. He helps us be kind and loving in all we do. He gives us mercy towards others, too. That means he helps us to love and want to help all people—even people who aren't very nice. That's part of being like Jesus. Let's sing "I Want to Be Like Jesus" as a prayer. Ask God to help you grow to be the person he wants you to be.

Sing "I Want to Be Like Jesus."
Lyrics and motions are in the back of this book.

PRAY Lord, we thank you for helping us grow. Without your help, we'd never become the people you want us to be. We'd never know you. We'd never grow up in our faith. But you help each step of the way. For all you do, Lord, we praise and worship you. Thank you, gracious Lord. In Jesus' name, amen.

The Right Fruit

Joy to the World!

Joy to the world! The Lord is come! ...... (Circle your forearms, beginning over your head and circling them down to waist level.)

Let earth receive her King! .... (Lift your palms higher on each word.)

Let every heart prepare him room. .... (Put both hands on your heart and tap them to the beat of the music.)

And heaven and nature sing. .... (Move your arms as if you're directing music.)
And heaven and nature sing,
And heaven, and heaven and nature sing.

"Joy to the World!" Arrangement © 2000 Group Publishing, Inc. All rights reserved.

Just Like You Promised

Just like you promised, you've come. .. (Put your hands together as if praying, then roll your hands toward your body.)

Just like you told us, you're here; .... (Move your cupped hands outward from your mouth, then point both index fingers down.)

And my desire is that you know ...... (Point to yourself, then point up.)

I love you, I worship you, ... (Hug yourself, point up, lift both arms up, then point up.)

I welcome you here. .... (With one hand, motion "Come.")

"Just Like You Promised" by Patty Marine. © 1982 Mercy/Vineyard Publishing/ASCAP. All rights reserved. International copyright secured. Used by permission.

To Save the World Through Him (John 3:17)

For God did not send his Son into the world .... (Stand so your right shoulder faces the children. Sway back and forth to the beat, and wag your finger "no.")

To condemn the world.
For God did not send his Son into the world .... (Jump and turn so your left shoulder faces the children. Sway back and forth to the beat, and wag your finger "no.")

To condemn the world, oh no,

But to save the world through him, ...(Sign "save" by crossing your fists in front of your chest, then uncrossing them and swinging your arms out to your side. Sign "world" by holding up three fingers on each hand, then circling the right hand around the left. Sign "through" by making the Vulcan greeting sign—spreading the third and fourth fingers of your left hand and passing your right hand through. For "him," point up.)

But to save the world through him. ...(Sign "save," "world," "through," and "him" again.)

For God did not send his Son into the world .... (Face front, and sway back and forth to the beat as you wag your finger "no.")

To condemn the world.

"To Save the World Through Him" (John 3:17) by Dean-o. © 2000 BibleBeat Music. Used by permission.

Mary's Boy Child

Long time ago in Bethlehem, ...(Point to your wrist, then indicate far away by pointing left with your thumb.)

So the Holy Bible say, ...(Open your hands as if they're a book.)
Mary's boy child, Jesus Christ, ...(Pretend to cradle a baby in your arms.)
Was born on Christmas day. ....(Form C's with both hands; place the C's in front of you, palms down; then turn palms up.)

Hark now, hear the angels sing. ....(Cup your ear with your hand.)
A new King born today ....(To sign "king," form a K by pointing up with the first two fingers of the left hand and putting the tip of the left thumb in the web between them. Move the K from your left shoulder to your right hip.)

That folks may live forevermore ....(Point to the children. Then sign "forever" by pointing to your temple then making a scooping motion out to the side; then, with fingers except thumb and pinkie folded in, move your hand in a downward scooping motion.)

Because of Christmas day. ....(Form C's with both hands; place the C's in front of you, palms down; then turn palms up.)

Now Joseph and his wife, Mary, ...(Extend first your left hand and then your right hand.)
Went to Bethlehem that night ....(Walk in place.)
And found no place to lay their head— (Pillow your head on your hands.)
Not a single room was in sight. ....(Wag finger "no.")

Hark now, hear the angels sing: ....(Cup your ear with your hand.)
A new King born today ....(Sign "king" by forming a K, then move the K from your left shoulder to your right hip.)

That folks may live forevermore ....(Point to the children; sign "forever" by pointing to your temple then making a scooping motion to the side; then, with fingers except thumb and pinkie folded in, make a downward scooping motion.)

Because of Christmas day. ....(Form C's with both hands; place the C's in front of you, palms down; then turn palms up.)

While shepherds watched their flocks by night, ...(Shade your eyes, and peer from side to side.)

They saw a bright, new, shining star........(Put your index fingers and thumbs together to form a triangle, and lift the triangle above your head; then separate your hands and lower your arms to your sides.)

And from the East there came three men ....(Point to the right with your thumb, then hold up three fingers.)

Bearing gifts from afar. ....(Make an exaggerated carrying motion.)

Hark now, hear the angels sing: ....(Cup your ear with your hand.)
A new King born today ....(Sign "king" by forming a K, then move the K from your left shoulder to your right hip.)

That folks may live forevermore ....(Point to the children; then sign "forever" by pointing to your temple then making a scooping motion out to the side; then, with fingers except thumb and pinkie folded in, move your hand in a downward scooping motion.)

Because of Christmas day. ....(Form C's with both hands; place the C's in front of you, palms down; then turn palms up.)

My God Is

My God is the God of creation. . . . . . .(Spread your arms wide, and turn around.)
My God made the land and the sea. . . .(Spread your arms to indicate flat land,
then make wave motions with your arm.)

My God gave me hope and salvation. . .(Raise your hands, first your left then
your right.)
Oh, that's what my God is to me. . . . .(Raise your hand, then point to yourself
with your thumb.)

Father, Savior—
Oh, that's what my God is to me, to me. .(Raise your hand, then point to yourself with
your thumb.)

Creator, master—
Oh, that's what my God is to me. . . . .(Raise your hand, then point to yourself
with your thumb.)

My God is a friend to the lonely. . . . . .(Pat a friend on the back.)
My God sets the prisoner free. . . . . . .(Cross your arms in front of your face,
then uncross them.)

My God is a loving companion. . . . . . .(Hug yourself.)
Oh, that's what my God is to me. . . . .(Raise your hand, then point to yourself
with your thumb.)

Joy!

I've got the joy, (joy), joy, (joy).
joy, (joy). . . . .(Raise your hands higher on each "joy.")
I got the joy, (joy), joy, (joy), joy, (joy).
I got the joy, (joy), joy, (joy).
joy...joy...joy. . . . .(On the last "joy," raise your arms to your
waist, then higher and higher.)
Two! Three! Four! . . . .(Count off the numbers on your fingers.)

Down in my heart, ...(Clap twice.)
Down in my heart, ...(Clap twice.)
Down in my heart to stay. . . . .(Dance in place.)
Down in my heart to stay. . . . .(Turn in your own circle between stanzas.)

I've got the love, (love), love, (love),
love, (love). . . . .(Raise your hands higher on each "love.")
I got the love, (love), love, (love),
love, (love),
I got the love, (love), love, (love),
love...love...love. . . . .(On the last "love," raise your arms to
your waist, then lift them higher and
higher.)
Two! Three! Four! . . . .(Count off the numbers on your fingers.)

I've got the light, (light), light, (light),
light, (light). . . . .(Raise hands higher on each "light.")
I got the light, (light), light, (light),
light, (light).
I got the light, (light), light, (light),
light...light...light. . . . .(On the last "light," raise your arms to
your waist, then lift them higher and
higher.)
Two! Three! Four! . . . .(Count off the numbers on your fingers.)

Praise, I Will Praise You, Lord

Praise, I will praise you, Lord, ...("Clap" silently.)
With all my heart. ....("Clap" silently.)
O God, I will tell the wonders of your
ways ....(Place your hands over your heart.)
And glorify your name. ....(Cup your hands around your mouth.)

Praise, I will praise you, Lord, ...(Make big circles with your hands, fluttering your fingers.)
With all my heart. ....("Clap" silently.)
In you I will find the source of all my joy. ....(Place your hands over your heart.)
                                                                          (Point up, then draw a smile on your face.)

Alleluia! ....("Clap" silently.)

Love, I will love you, Lord, ...(Place your hands over your heart.)
With all my heart. ....(Place your hands over your heart.)
O God, I will tell the wonders of your
ways ....(Hold your hands over your heart.)
And glorify your name. ....(Cup your hands around your mouth.)

Love, I will love you, Lord, ...(Make big circles with your hands, fluttering your fingers.)
With all my heart. ....(Place your hands over your heart.)
In you I will find the source of all my joy. ....(Hold your hands over your heart.)
                                                                          (Point up, then draw a smile on your face.)

Alleluia! ....("Clap" silently.)

Serve, I will serve you, Lord, ...(Place your hands in front of you.)
With all my heart. ....(Place your hands over your heart.)
O God, I will tell the wonders of your
ways ....(Cup your hands around your mouth.)
And glorify your name. ....(Make big circles with your hands, fluttering your fingers.)

Serve, I will serve you, Lord, ...(Place your hands in front of you.)
With all my heart. ....(Place your hands over your heart.)
In you I will find the source of all my joy. ....(Point up, then draw a smile on your face.)

Alleluia! ....("Clap" silently.)

Jesus Loves Me Rock

Jesus loves me ....(Sign "love.")
This I know, ...(Point to head with both hands.)
For the Bible ....(Make a book.)
Tells me so. ....(Point to self with both hands.)

Little children ....(Hold hands out, palms facing down.)
To him belong. ....(Raise arms.)
They are weak, but ....(Swing arms from side to side)
He's so strong! ....(Flex both arms.)

Jaaaayy! ....(Cup hands around mouth.)
Eeeeeee! ....(Cup hands around mouth.)
Sssssssss-aaaah! ....(Bend arms at elbows. Swing them back and forth.)
Uuuuuuu! ....(Raise arms.)
Sssssssss-aaaah! ....(Bend arms at elbows. Swing them back and forth.)

And what's that spell? ....(Cup hands around mouth.)
Jesus! ....(Raise both fists.)
And who do you love? ....(Cup hands around mouth.)
Jesus! ....(Raise both arms.)
And who loves you? ....(Cup hands around mouth.)
Jesus! ....(Raise both arms.)
Who died for you? ....(Cup hands around mouth.)
Jesus! ....(Raise both arms.)
And who's your guy? ....(Cup hands around mouth.)
Jesus! ....(Raise both arms.)
The apple of your eye! ....(Cup hands around mouth.)
Jesus! ....(Raise both arms.)
And who's your friend? ....(Cup hands around mouth.)
Jesus! ....(Raise both arms.)
He'll love ya to the end! ....(Cup hands around mouth.)

Jesus Is Lord of All

Lyrics	Motions
Jesus is Lord of all.	(Sign "Jesus" by pointing to each palm with the index finger of the opposite hand. Sign "Lord" by making an L with the thumb and index finger of the right hand and moving it from the left shoulder to the right hip.)
Jesus is Lord of all.	(Sign "Jesus," then sign "Lord.")
No sin is too big,	(Extend your arms wide.)
No problem too small;	(Hold your thumb and index finger close together to indicate something small.)
Jesus is Lord of all.	(Sign "Jesus," then sign "Lord.")
Jesus is King of kings.	(Sign "Jesus," then sign "Lord.")
My Lord is King of kings.	(Sign "Jesus," then sign "Lord.")
Presidents, princes, paupers will sing,	
"Jesus is King of kings."	(Sign "Jesus," then sign "Lord.")
Jesus Christ is Lord of all,	(Sign "Jesus," then sign "Lord.")
King of kings and Lord of lords.	(Sign "king," then sign "Lord.")
You know he's Lord of all.	(Point to the children, sign "Lord," then extend your arms wide.)
Jesus is coming soon.	(Roll your arms from above your head to waist level.)
Jesus is coming soon.	(Roll your arms from above your head to waist level.)
Just look in your heart and see if there's room.	(Shade your eyes, "draw" a heart on your chest with your finger, then shade your eyes.)
'Cause Jesus is coming soon.	(Roll your arms from above your head to waist level.)

"Jesus Is Lord of All" by Keith Green. © 1982 Birdwing Music/BMG Songs/ASCAP. All rights reserved. Used by permission.

He Is Really God

Lyrics	Motions
He's more than a prophet	(Raise your left arm.)
Or just a man.	(Raise your right arm.)
He makes his home	(Point up.)
Up in glory land.	(Flutter your hands as you lift them high.)
He came from the Father	(Circle your forearms, starting up high and moving down to waist level.)
Just to lend us all a hand.	(Shake hands with a person next to you.)
Shazam and Superman	(Make a muscle with your left arm.)
Are real tough dudes,	(Make a muscle with your right arm.)
But they don't come sportin'	(Wag your finger.)
What Jesus do.	(Point up.)
He came from the Father;	(Circle your forearms, starting up high and moving down to waist level.)
To the Father he was true.	(Circle your forearms back up.)
I know that he is really God.	(Tap your temple, then point up.)
He made it all	(Spread your arms wide.)
And holds together everything.	(Clasp your hands in front of your face.)
I know that he's the one—	(Tap your temple, then point up.)
The Father's one and only Son.	(Raise your hands.)
I know that he is really God.	(Tap your temple, then point up.)
He is really God!	(Clap to the beat.)

"He Is Really God" by Dean-o. © 1997 FKO Music, Inc. All rights reserved. Used by permission.

We Believe in God

We believe in God, ... (Raise your right hand; then bend your right elbow to bring your hand to shoulder height.)

And we all need Jesus, ... (Sign "Jesus" by pointing to each palm with the middle finger of the opposite hand.)

'Cause life is hard, ... (Pat another person on the back.)

And it might not get easier. .... (Pat another person on the back.)

But don't be afraid .... ("Tremble" hands in front of yourself.)

To know who you are, ... (Point to your head.)

And don't be afraid to show it. .... ("Tremble" your hands in front of yourself.)

If you believe in God, ... (Spread your arms wide.)

If you say you need Jesus, ... (Sign "Jesus.")

He'll be where you are, ... (Sign "Jesus.")

And he never will leave you. .... (Pat another person's back.)

Sing to me now .... (Cup your hands around your mouth.)

Words that are true, ... (Make a thumbs-up sign.)

So all in this place can know it. .... (Spread arms wide and point to head.)

We believe in God. .... (Raise your right hand; then bend your right elbow to bring your hand to shoulder height.)

And we all need Jesus. .... (Sign "Jesus.")

We believe in God. .... (Raise your right hand; then bend your right elbow to bring your hand to shoulder height.)

And we all need Jesus. .... (Sign "Jesus.")

We believe in God. .... (Raise your right hand; then bend your right elbow to bring your hand to shoulder height.)

And we all need Jesus. .... (Sign "Jesus.")

His Love

His love is higher than the highest of mountains. .... (Stand on your toes and make an over-
hand scooping motion as high as you can reach.)

His love goes deeper than the deepest of seas. .... (Squat and make an underhand scooping motion as low as you can go.)

His love, it stretches to the farthest horizon. .... (Put your hands in front of your chest and make a stretching motion, as if pulling taffy.)

His love, his mighty love, it reaches to me. .... (Point up, then roll your forearms from high up down to your chest. Point to yourself.)

His love is stronger than the angels and demons. .... (Make flying motions, then hold your fists in front of yourself and tremble as if in fear.)

His love, it keeps me in my life's darkest hour. .... (Hug yourself, then cover your eyes.)

His love secures me on the pathway to heaven. .... (Walk your hands upward toward heaven.)

His love, oh, his mighty love, is my strength and power. .... (Point up, and hug yourself. "Make a muscle" with your left arm, then "make a muscle" with your right arm.)

The Good Life

This is the good, good life. .... (Lean left, then clap; lean right, then clap.
Lean left, then clap; lean right, then clap.)
God loves me—this I know. .... (Hug yourself, then point to your head.)
This is the good, good life. .... (Lean left, then clap; lean right, then clap.
Lean left, then clap; lean right, then clap.)
God loves me, and I let it show. ...... (Open your arms wide, then twirl around.)

We're here together; .... (Put your arms around each other, then
lean from left to right.)
Friends are all around. .... (Continue leaning left and right.)
Jesus Christ loves us all, so we ...... (Continue leaning left and right.)
Make a great big sound. .... (Shout.)
The ocean and the mountains, ... (Move your hands in wave-like motions
toward each other, then place the tips of
your fingers together to suggest a
mountain peak.)
The trees and the stars, ... (Show straight-up-and-down hands with
palms together, then "twinkle" your fin-
gers in the air.)
They show us God .... (Continue to "twinkle" your fingers.)
Is a great big God, ... (Spread your arms wide.)
Yet he still knows who we are. ...... (Point to yourself with your thumbs.)

This is the good, good life. .... (Lean left, then clap; lean right, then clap.
Lean left, then clap; lean right, then clap.)
God loves me—this I know. .... (Hug yourself, then point to your head.)
This is the good, good life. .... (Lean left, then clap; lean right, then clap.
Lean left, then clap; lean right, then clap.)
God loves me, and I let it show. ...... (Open your arms wide, then twirl around.)

Look around and see your family, ... (Shade your eyes, and look around.)
'Cause Jesus made us all one bunch .. (Show one index finger.)
When he came to set us free. .... (Cross your wrists, then open your arms.)
Life is exciting, so we dance and
celebrate. .... (Open your arms wide, then twirl around.)
Yeah, sing your praises to the Lord— . (Clap your hands.)
Oh Lord, you are so great. .... (Lift your hands to God.)

This is the good, good life. .... (Lean left, then clap; lean right, then clap.
Lean left, then clap; lean right, then clap.)
God loves me—this I know. .... (Hug yourself, then point to your head.)
This is the good, good life. .... (Lean left, then clap; lean right, then clap.
Lean left, then clap; lean right, then clap.)
God loves me, and I let it show. ...... (Open your arms wide, then twirl around.)

Seek Ye First

Seek ye first the kingdom of God .... (Shade your eyes with your hand.)
And his righteousness, ... (Point to the ceiling.)
And all these things shall be added
unto you. .... (Put your hands in front of you as if
you're being handed a gift.)
Allelu, alleluia! .... (Circle your right fist above your head.)

Ask and it shall be given unto you; .. (Extend one hand, palm up, in front of
you, then cover it with the other hand.)
Seek and you shall find; .... (Shade your eyes with your hand.)
Knock and the door shall be opened
unto you. .... (Make a knocking motion.)
Allelu, alleluia!
Allelu, alleluia! .... (Circle your right fist above your head.)

Rise Up and Praise Him

Let the heavens rejoice. ....(Hold your hands high, and wave them back and forth.)

Let the earth be glad. ....(Hold your hands low, and wave them back and forth.)

Let the people of God ....(Clap to the beat.)

Sing his praise ....(Clap to the beat.)

All over the land. ....(Turn around while clapping.)

Everyone in the valley, ...(Hold your hands and arms in a V shape.)

Come and lift your voice. ....(Beckon with your arm, then cup your hands around your mouth.)

All those on the mountaintop be glad. .(Place your palms together overhead to suggest a mountain.)

Shout for joy. ....(Punch your fists in the air on each word.)

Rise up and praise him. ....(Jump, then clap to the beat.)

He deserves our love. ....(Do a freestyle action.)

Rise up and praise him. ....(Jump, then clap to the beat.)

Worship the holy one ....(Do a freestyle action.)

With all your heart, ...(Place your hands on your heart.)

With all your soul, ...(Point to your mind.)

With all your might. ....("Make muscles.")

Rise up and praise him. ....(Jump, then clap to the beat.)

"Rise Up and Praise Him" by Gary Sadler and Paul Baloche. © 1996 Integrity's Hosanna! Music/ASCAP. All rights reserved. Used by permission.

Hear, Oh Israel (Deuteronomy 6:4–5)

Hear, oh Israel, the Lord our God is one Lord. ....(Cup your ears. Then lift your hands. Hold up your index finger on "one.")

You shall love the Lord your God with all of your heart. ....(Grapevine to the right twice. Then draw a heart on your chest with your index fingers.)

You shall love the Lord your God with all of your soul. ....(Grapevine to the left twice. Then make an O with your left hand, and bring your right-hand index finger and thumb together so you can pretend to pull something from inside the left-hand O.)

You shall love the Lord your God with all of your mind. ....(Grapevine to the right twice. Then point to your temple.)

You shall love the Lord your God with all of your strength. ....(Grapevine to the left twice. Then "make muscles" with both arms.)

"Hear, Oh Israel" (Deuteronomy 6:4–5). Arrangement © 1994/2000 Group Publishing, Inc. All rights reserved.

I Want to Be Like Jesus

I want to be like Jesus. ....(Sign "I" by holding your fist to your chest and extending your pinky up. Sign "want" by extending your forearms, palms up, and pulling your arms toward yourself while making a grabbing motion with your fingers. Sign "to" by touching index fingers. Sign "be" by holding fingers straight up, crossing your thumb across your palm, and holding your hand against your chin. Sign "like" by making an L-shape with your thumb and index finger, holding the L on your chest, and, as you draw your hand away from your chest, closing your thumb and forefinger. Sign "Jesus" by touching the middle finger of each hand to the opposite palm.)

I want to be like Jesus. ....(Sign "I want to be like Jesus.")
I want to be like Jesus. ....(Sign "I want to be like Jesus.")
I want to be like Jesus. ....(Sign "I want to be like Jesus.")

Grant me a heart that's pure and true. (echo) ....("Draw" a heart on your chest with your index finger.)

Kind and loving in all I do. (echo) ....(Make K's with both hands, circle them vertically, then cross your arms on your chest.)

Full of mercy for all who come (echo) ..(Spread your arms wide, then roll your forearms from above your head to your waist.)

Running into the Father's arms. (echo) ..(Run in place, then lift your arms up.)

I want to be like Jesus. ....(Sign "I want to be like Jesus.")
I want to be like Jesus. ....(Sign "I want to be like Jesus.")
I want to be like Jesus. ....(Sign "I want to be like Jesus.")
I want to be like Jesus. ....(Sign "I want to be like Jesus.")

I want eyes that see you. (echo) ....(Make a V with your first two fingers. Point to your eyes, then lift the V toward heaven.)

Ears that hear from you. (echo) ......(Cup your ear, then lift your cupped hand to heaven.)

Feet that follow after you; (echo) ....(Point to your feet, then walk around in your area.)

I want to be just like you. (echo) ......(Sign "I want to be just like you." To sign "just," hold your index finger straight up in the air and twist your hand.)

I want (echo) ....(Sign "I want.")
To be (echo) ....(Sign "to be.")
Just like (echo) ....(Sign "just like.")
Jesus. (echo) ....(Sign "Jesus.")

I want to be like Jesus. ....(Sign "I want to be like Jesus.")
I want to be like Jesus. ....(Sign "I want to be like Jesus.")
I want to be like Jesus. ....(Sign "I want to be like Jesus.")
I want to be like Jesus. ....(Sign "I want to be like Jesus.")
I want to be like Jesus. ....(Sign "I want to be like Jesus.")

Love With the Love of Jesus

Love with the love that can only
be Jesus. ....(Cross your arms on your chest, then
    sign "Jesus" by pointing to each palm
    with the index finger of the opposite
    hand.)

Love with the love that goes so
deep: Jesus. ....(Cross your arms on your chest, bend
    your knees on "deep," then sign "Jesus.")

Oh, serve the Lord with gladness .....(On "serve," hold your hands in front of
    you, palms up, and move hands back and
    forth alternately. On "gladness," hold
    right palm with fingers pointing left, and
    bring it from waist to chest level, moving
    the palm upward and outward.)

And honor others, too. ....(Pat a neighbor on the back.)

In everything, Lord, make me
more like you. ....(Extend your arms out, then raise your
    hands to heaven.)

I Love You, Lord

I love you, Lord, ...(Hug yourself.)

And I lift my voice ....(Make a V shape with your right index and
    middle fingers, then move those finger-
    tips along your throat and up toward the
    ceiling.)

To worship you: ....("Clap" silently while you look up.)

O my soul rejoice. ....(Pat your right hand over your chest to
    symbolize a quickly beating heart.)

Take joy, my King, in what you hear; ..(Above your head, make a "crown" by
    making a circle with your index fingers
    and thumbs.)

May it be a sweet, sweet sound in
your ear. ....(Cup your hand behind your ear.)

I love you, Lord, ...(Hug yourself.)

And I lift my voice ....(Make a V shape with your right index and
    middle fingers, then move those finger-
    tips along your throat and up toward the
    ceiling.)

To worship you: ....("Clap" silently while you look up.)

O my soul rejoice. ....(Pat your right hand over your chest to
    symbolize a quickly beating heart.)

Take joy, my King, in what you hear; .(Above your head, make a "crown" by
    making a circle with your index fingers
    and thumbs.)

May it be a sweet sound in your ear. ......(Cup your hand behind your ear.)

Your Everlasting Love

(Do jumping jacks to the beat, clapping after each jack, before the song and between the verses.)

Your everlasting love is higher, ...(Hug yourself, then extend your hands on "higher.")

Higher, higher than the sky. ....(Raise your hands on each "higher," then wave your hands back and forth above head.)

Your everlasting love is higher, ...(Hug yourself, then extend your hands on "higher.")

Higher, higher than the sky, ...(Raise your hands on each "higher," then wave your hands back and forth above your head.)

Higher than the sky. ....(Wave your hands back and forth above your head.)

All the wonder of your everlasting love ....(Roll your arms to the left, then to the right.)

Is higher than the sky. ....(Wave your hands back and forth above your head.)

Your everlasting love is deeper, ...(Hug yourself, then bend at the knees.)

Deeper, deeper than the sea. ....(Bend a little more on each "deeper.")

Your everlasting love is deeper, ...(Hug yourself, then bend at the knees.)

Deeper, deeper than the sea. ....(Bend a little more on each "deeper.")

Deeper than the sea. ....(Stand up, then bend down.)

All the wonder of your everlasting love ....(Roll your arms to the left, then to the right.)

Is deeper than the sea. ....(Bend at the knees.)

Higher than the heavens above ....(Wave your hands back and forth above your head.)

Is the glory of your wonderful love. ..(Shake your hands above your head, then hug yourself.)

I'm lost in the mystery of ....(Put your hands over your eyes.)

Your everlasting love, ...(Raise your hands wide above your head, then hug yourself.)

Your everlasting love. ....(Raise your hands wide above your head, then hug yourself.)

Your everlasting love, ...(Raise your hands wide above your head, then hug yourself.)

Your everlasting love. ....(Raise your hands wide above your head, then hug yourself.)

Your everlasting love is reaching. ....(Hug yourself, then extend your hand straight out in front.)

Reaching, reaching out to me. ....(Reach your hand out farther on each "reaching.")

Your everlasting love is reaching, ...(Hug yourself, then extend your hand straight out in front.)

Reaching, reaching out to me. ....(Reach your hand out farther on each "reaching.")

Reaching out to me ....(Reach your hand out even further.)

All the wonder of your everlasting love ....(Roll your arms to the left, then to the right.)

Is reaching out to me. ....(Reach your hand out in front of yourself.)

We Want to See Jesus Lifted High

We want to see Jesus lifted high, ...(Lift your hands.)

A banner that flies across this land ...(Wave your hands back and forth above your head.)

That all men might see the truth
and know ....(Shade eyes, and peer from side to side.)

He is the way to heaven. ....(Point your index finger up, and move it from waist level to above your head.)

We want to see, we want to see, ...(Shade your eyes and look left. Shade your eyes and look right.)

We want to see Jesus lifted high. ....(Sign "Jesus" by pointing to each palm with the index finger of the opposite hand, then make a lifting motion.)

We want to see, we want to see, ...(Shade your eyes and look left. Shade your eyes and look right.)

We want to see Jesus lifted high. .....(Sign "Jesus," then make a lifting motion.)

"We Want to See Jesus Lifted High" by Doug Horley. © 1993 Kingsway's Thankyou Music/PRS. All rights in the Western Hemisphere administered by EMI Christian Music Publishing. All rights reserved. Used by permission.

That You May Believe (John 20:31)

But these are written that you
may believe ....(Mime writing with your index finger.)

That Jesus is the Christ, the Son
of God, ...(Sign "Jesus" by pointing to each palm with the index finger of the opposite hand. Sign "Christ" by forming a C with your left hand and moving it from your left shoulder to your right hip. Sign "God" by drawing a vertical line in front of your face with your open hand, palm facing left.)

But these are written that you
may believe ....(Mime writing with your index finger.)

That Jesus is the Christ, the Son
of God, ...(Sign "Jesus," sign "Christ," then sign "God!")

And that by believing you may have
life in his name. ....(Sign "believe" by pointing to your temple, then clasping your hands together. Sign "life" by making L's with the thumbs and index fingers of both hands and making a scooping motion in front of your belly. Point up to indicate Jesus.)

And that by believing you may have
life in his name. ....(Repeat above motion.)

And that by believing you may have
life in his name, ...(Repeat above motion.)

And that by believing you may have
life in his name. ....(Repeat above motion.)

"That You May Believe" (John 20:31) by Dean-o. © 2000 BibleBeat Music. All rights reserved. Used by permission.

For to Us a Child Is Born (Isaiah 9:6)

For to us a child is born, to us a son is given. .... *(Pretend to cradle a baby in your arms, then pat the air as if patting a child's head.)*

And the government will be on his shoulders. .... *(Tap your shoulders.)*

For to us a child is born, to us a son is given. .... *(Pretend to cradle baby in your arms, then pat the air as if patting a child's head.)*

And the government will be on his shoulders. .... *(Tap your shoulders.)*

And he will be called Wonderful Counselor. .... *(Cup your hands around your mouth. Then, for "wonderful," pat the air in front of you twice with palms held out. For "Counselor," put your arm around someone's shoulders.)*

Mighty God, Everlasting Father, Prince of Peace. .... *("Make muscles," then sign "God" by drawing a line in front of your face with your right hand held with palm facing left. Sign "everlasting" by hooking your index finger from your temple outward, then form a fist with your index finger and thumb and move it away from your body, swooping down a bit. Sign "Father" by spreading the fingers of your right hand wide and putting your thumb to your forehead. Sign "Prince" by making a P (see illustration), and moving it from your left shoulder to your right hip. Sign "Peace" by crossing your palms in front of your chest and moving your palms downward and outward to shoulder width.)*

P

And he will be called Wonderful Counselor. .... *(Cup your hands around your mouth. Then, for "wonderful," pat the air in front of you twice with palms held out. For "Counselor," put your arm around someone's shoulders.)*

Mighty God, Everlasting Father, Prince of Peace. .... *("Make muscles," sign "God," sign "everlasting," sign "Father," sign "Prince," then sign "Peace.")*

Let Your Light Shine (Matthew 5:16)

(Throughout, sway back and forth to the beat.)

Let your light shine before men, that .. *(Hold up one finger to represent "light." Then flutter the fingers of both hands above your head and out to your sides.)*

They may see your good deeds and .. *(Shade your eyes, and look from left to right.)*

Praise your Father in heaven. .... *("Clap" your hands silently, then raise them up.)*

Let your light shine before men, yeah, *(Hold up one finger to represent "light." Then flutter the fingers of both hands above your head and out to your sides.)*

Let your light shine before men. ...... *(Hold up one finger to represent "light." Then flutter the fingers of both hands above your head and out to your sides.)*

Do to Others (Luke 6:31)

Do to others ....(Pat a friend's back.)
As you would have them do to you. ...(Pat your own back.)
Do to others ....(Pat a friend's back.)
As you would have them do. ....(Pat your own back.)

Be kind to one another, ...(Put your arms around your neighbor's
                                                                        shoulders.)
For this is the best way. ....(Give a thumbs-up sign.)
Love your sister and your brother. ....(Point to several children.)
Choose the right words to say. ....(Cup both hands around your mouth.)

As Jesus would do, ...(Point up.)
As you would have them do, ...(Pat your own back.)
As Jesus would do. ....(Point up.)

"Do to Others" (Luke 6:31) by Mary Rice Hopkins. © 1998 Big Steps 4 U (administered by Music
Services)/ASCAP. All rights reserved. Used by permission.